Love's Labour's Lost

Love's Labour's Lost

William Shakespeare

MINT EDITIONS

Love's Labour's Lost was first published in 1598.

This edition published by Mint Editions 2021.

ISBN 9781513136899 | E-ISBN 9781513210667

Published by Mint Editions®

MINT EDITIONS

minteditionbooks.com

Publishing Director: Jennifer Newens
Design & Production: Rachel Lopez Metzger
Project Manager: Micaela Clark
Typesetting: Westchester Publishing Services

Contents

Act V

Dramatis Personae

FERDINAND, King of Navarre
BEROWNE, lord attending on the King
LONGAVILLE, lord attending on the King
DUMAIN, lord attending on the King
BOYET, lord attending on the Princess of France
MARCADE, lord attending on the Princess of France
DON ADRIANO DE ARMADO, fantastical Spaniard
SIR NATHANIEL, a curate
HOLOFERNES, a schoolmaster
DULL, a constable
COSTARD, a clown
MOTH, page to Armado
A FORESTER

THE PRINCESS OF FRANCE
ROSALINE, lady attending on the Princess
MARIA, lord attending on the Princess
KATHARINE, lady attending on the Princess
JAQUENETTA, a country wench

Lords, Attendants, etc.

ACT I

Scene I

Navarre. The King's park

(*Enter the King,* BEROWNE, LONGAVILLE, *and* DUMAIN)

KING: Let fame, that all hunt after in their lives,
    Live regist'red upon our brazen tombs,
    And then grace us in the disgrace of death;
    When, spite of cormorant devouring Time,
    Th' endeavour of this present breath may buy
    That honour which shall bate his scythe's keen edge,
    And make us heirs of all eternity.
    Therefore, brave conquerors—for so you are
    That war against your own affections
    And the huge army of the world's desires—
    Our late edict shall strongly stand in force:
    Navarre shall be the wonder of the world;
    Our court shall be a little Academe,
    Still and contemplative in living art.
    You three, Berowne, Dumain, and Longaville,
    Have sworn for three years' term to live with me
    My fellow-scholars, and to keep those statutes
    That are recorded in this schedule here.
    Your oaths are pass'd; and now subscribe your names,
    That his own hand may strike his honour down
    That violates the smallest branch herein.
    If you are arm'd to do as sworn to do,
    Subscribe to your deep oaths, and keep it too.
LONGAVILLE: I am resolv'd; 'tis but a three years' fast.
    The mind shall banquet, though the body pine.
    Fat paunches have lean pates; and dainty bits
    Make rich the ribs, but bankrupt quite the wits.
DUMAIN: My loving lord, Dumain is mortified.
    The grosser manner of these world's delights
    He throws upon the gross world's baser slaves;
    To love, to wealth, to pomp, I pine and die,
    With all these living in philosophy.

BEROWNE: I can but say their protestation over;
    So much, dear liege, I have already sworn,
    That is, to live and study here three years.
    But there are other strict observances,
    As: not to see a woman in that term,
    Which I hope well is not enrolled there;
    And one day in a week to touch no food,
    And but one meal on everyday beside,
    The which I hope is not enrolled there;
    And then to sleep but three hours in the night
    And not be seen to wink of all the day—
    When I was wont to think no harm all night,
    And make a dark night too of half the day—
    Which I hope well is not enrolled there.
    O, these are barren tasks, too hard to keep,
    Not to see ladies, study, fast, not sleep!
KING: Your oath is pass'd to pass away from these.
BEROWNE: Let me say no, my liege, an if you please:
    I only swore to study with your Grace,
    And stay here in your court for three years' space.
LONGAVILLE: You swore to that, Berowne, and to the rest.
BEROWNE: By yea and nay, sir, then I swore in jest.
    What is the end of study, let me know.
KING: Why, that to know which else we should not know.
BEROWNE: Things hid and barr'd, you mean, from common sense?
KING: Ay, that is study's god-like recompense.
BEROWNE: Come on, then; I will swear to study so,
    To know the thing I am forbid to know,
    As thus: to study where I well may dine,
    When I to feast expressly am forbid;
    Or study where to meet some mistress fine,
    When mistresses from common sense are hid;
    Or, having sworn too hard-a-keeping oath,
    Study to break it, and not break my troth.
    If study's gain be thus, and this be so,
    Study knows that which yet it doth not know.
    Swear me to this, and I will ne'er say no.
KING: These be the stops that hinder study quite,
    And train our intellects to vain delight.

BEROWNE: Why, all delights are vain; but that most vain
    Which, with pain purchas'd, doth inherit pain,
    As painfully to pore upon a book
    To seek the light of truth; while truth the while
    Doth falsely blind the eyesight of his look.
    Light, seeking light, doth light of light beguile;
    So, ere you find where light in darkness lies,
    Your light grows dark by losing of your eyes.
    Study me how to please the eye indeed,
    By fixing it upon a fairer eye;
    Who dazzling so, that eye shall be his heed,
    And give him light that it was blinded by.
    Study is like the heaven's glorious sun,
    That will not be deep-search'd with saucy looks;
    Small have continual plodders ever won,
    Save base authority from others' books.
    These earthly godfathers of heaven's lights
    That give a name to every fixed star
    Have no more profit of their shining nights
    Than those that walk and wot not what they are.
    Too much to know is to know nought but fame;
    And every godfather can give a name.
KING: How well he's read, to reason against reading!
DUMAIN: Proceeded well, to stop all good proceeding!
LONGAVILLE: He weeds the corn, and still lets grow the weeding.
BEROWNE: The spring is near, when green geese are a-breeding.
DUMAIN: How follows that?
BEROWNE: Fit in his place and time.
DUMAIN: In reason nothing.
BEROWNE: Something then in rhyme.
LONGAVILLE: Berowne is like an envious sneaping frost
    That bites the first-born infants of the spring.
BEROWNE: Well, say I am; why should proud summer boast
    Before the birds have any cause to sing?
    Why should I joy in any abortive birth?
    At Christmas I no more desire a rose
    Than wish a snow in May's new-fangled shows;
    But like of each thing that in season grows;
    So you, to study now it is too late,

Climb o'er the house to unlock the little gate.

KING: Well, sit out; go home, Berowne; adieu.

BEROWNE: No, my good lord; I have sworn to stay with you;
And though I have for barbarism spoke more
Than for that angel knowledge you can say,
Yet confident I'll keep what I have swore,
And bide the penance of each three years' day.
Give me the paper; let me read the same;
And to the strictest decrees I'll write my name.

KING: How well this yielding rescues thee from shame!

BEROWNE: (*Reads*) "Item. That no woman shall come within a mile of
my court"—Hath this been proclaimed?

LONGAVILLE: Four days ago.

BEROWNE: Let's see the penalty. (*Reads*) "—on pain of losing her
tongue." Who devis'd this penalty?

LONGAVILLE: Marry, that did I.

BEROWNE: Sweet lord, and why?

LONGAVILLE: To fright them hence with that dread penalty.

BEROWNE: A dangerous law against gentility.
        (*Reads*) "Item. If any man be seen to talk with a woman
within the term of three years, he shall endure such public
shame as the rest of the court can possibly devise."
This article, my liege, yourself must break;
For well you know here comes in embassy
The French king's daughter, with yourself to speak—
A mild of grace and complete majesty—
About surrender up of Aquitaine
To her decrepit, sick, and bedrid father;
Therefore this article is made in vain,
Or vainly comes th' admired princess hither.

KING: What say you, lords? Why, this was quite forgot.

BEROWNE: So study evermore is over-shot.
While it doth study to have what it would,
It doth forget to do the thing it should;
And when it hath the thing it hunteth most,
'Tis won as towns with fire—so won, so lost.

KING: We must of force dispense with this decree;
She must lie here on mere necessity.

BEROWNE: Necessity will make us all forsworn

Three thousand times within this three years' space;
For every man with his affects is born,
Not by might mast'red, but by special grace.
If I break faith, this word shall speak for me:
I am forsworn on mere necessity.
So to the laws at large I write my name;

(Subscribes)

And he that breaks them in the least degree
Stands in attainder of eternal shame.
Suggestions are to other as to me;
But I believe, although I seem so loath,
I am the last that will last keep his oath.
But is there no quick recreation granted?
KING: Ay, that there is. Our court, you know, is haunted
With a refined traveller of Spain,
A man in all the world's new fashion planted,
That hath a mint of phrases in his brain;
One who the music of his own vain tongue
Doth ravish like enchanting harmony;
A man of complements, whom right and wrong
Have chose as umpire of their mutiny.
This child of fancy, that Armado hight,
For interim to our studies shall relate,
In high-born words, the worth of many a knight
From tawny Spain lost in the world's debate.
How you delight, my lords, I know not, I;
But I protest I love to hear him lie,
And I will use him for my minstrelsy.
BEROWNE: Armado is a most illustrious wight,
A man of fire-new words, fashion's own knight.
LONGAVILLE: Costard the swain and he shall be our sport;
And so to study three years is but short.
(Enter DULL, *a constable, with a letter, and* COSTARD)
DULL: Which is the Duke's own person?
BEROWNE: This, fellow. What wouldst?
DULL: I myself reprehend his own person, for I am his Grace's
farborough; but I would see his own person in flesh and
blood.
BEROWNE: This is he.

DULL: Signior Arme—Arme—commends you. There's villainy abroad; this letter will tell you more.

COSTARD: Sir, the contempts thereof are as touching me.

KING: A letter from the magnificent Armado.

BEROWNE: How low soever the matter, I hope in God for high words.

LONGAVILLE: A high hope for a low heaven. God grant us patience!

BEROWNE: To hear, or forbear hearing?

LONGAVILLE: To hear meekly, sir, and to laugh moderately; or, to forbear both.

BEROWNE: Well, sir, be it as the style shall give us cause to climb in the merriness.

COSTARD: The matter is to me, sir, as concerning Jaquenetta. The manner of it is, I was taken with the manner.

BEROWNE: In what manner?

COSTARD: In manner and form following, sir; all those three: I was seen with her in the manor-house, sitting with her upon the form, and taken following her into the park; which, put together, is in manner and form following. Now, sir, for the manner—it is the manner of a man to speak to a woman. For the form—in some form.

BEROWNE: For the following, sir?

COSTARD: As it shall follow in my correction; and God defend the right!

KING: Will you hear this letter with attention?

BEROWNE: As we would hear an oracle.

COSTARD: Such is the simplicity of man to hearken after the flesh.

KING: (*Reads*) "Great deputy, the welkin's vicegerent and sole dominator of Navarre, my soul's earth's god and body's fost'ring patron"—

COSTARD: Not a word of Costard yet.

KING: (*Reads*) "So it is"—

COSTARD: It may be so; but if he say it is so, he is, in telling true, but so.

KING: Peace!

COSTARD: Be to me, and every man that dares not fight!

KING: No words!

COSTARD: Of other men's secrets, I beseech you.

KING: (*Reads*) "So it is, besieged with sable-coloured melancholy, I did commend the black oppressing humour to the most wholesome physic of thy health-giving air; and, as I am a gentleman, betook myself to walk. The time When? About the sixth hour; when beasts most graze, birds best peck, and men sit down to that nourishment which is called supper. So much for the time When. Now for the ground Which? which, I mean, I upon; it is ycleped thy park. Then for the place Where? where, I mean, I did encounter that obscene and most prepost'rous event that draweth from my snow-white pen the ebon-coloured ink which here thou viewest, beholdest, surveyest, or seest. But to the place Where? It standeth north-north-east and by east from the west corner of thy curious-knotted garden. There did I see that low-spirited swain, that base minnow of thy mirth,"

COSTARD: Me?

KING: "that unlettered small-knowing soul,"

COSTARD: Me?

KING: "that shallow vassal,"

COSTARD: Still me?

KING: "which, as I remember, hight Costard,"

COSTARD: O, me!

KING: "sorted and consorted, contrary to thy established proclaimed edict and continent canon; which, with, O, with—but with this I passion to say wherewith—"

COSTARD: With a wench. King. "with a child of our grandmother Eve, a female; or, for thy more sweet understanding, a woman. Him I, as my ever-esteemed duty pricks me on, have sent to thee, to receive the meed of punishment, by thy sweet Grace's officer, Antony Dull, a man of good repute, carriage, bearing, and estimation."

DULL: Me, an't shall please you; I am Antony Dull.

KING: "For Jaquenetta—so is the weaker vessel called, which I apprehended with the aforesaid swain—I keep her as a vessel of thy law's fury; and shall, at the least of thy sweet notice, bring her to trial. Thine, in all compliments of devoted and heart-burning heat of duty, DON ADRIANO DE ARMADO."

BEROWNE: This is not so well as I look'd for, but the best that ever I heard.

KING: Ay, the best for the worst. But, sirrah, what say you to this?

COSTARD: Sir, I confess the wench.

KING: Did you hear the proclamation?

COSTARD: I do confess much of the hearing it, but little of the marking of it.

KING: It was proclaimed a year's imprisonment to be taken with a wench.

COSTARD: I was taken with none, sir; I was taken with a damsel.

KING: Well, it was proclaimed damsel.

COSTARD: This was no damsel neither, sir; she was a virgin.

KING: It is so varied too, for it was proclaimed virgin.

COSTARD: If it were, I deny her virginity; I was taken with a maid.

KING: This "maid" not serve your turn, sir.

COSTARD: This maid will serve my turn, sir.

KING: Sir, I will pronounce your sentence: you shall fast a week with bran and water.

COSTARD: I had rather pray a month with mutton and porridge.

KING: And Don Armado shall be your keeper.
My Lord Berowne, see him delivered o'er;
And go we, lords, to put in practice that
Which each to other hath so strongly sworn.

(*Exeunt* KING, LONGAVILLE, *and* DUMAIN)

BEROWNE: I'll lay my head to any good man's hat
These oaths and laws will prove an idle scorn.
Sirrah, come on.

COSTARD: I suffer for the truth, sir; for true it is I was taken with Jaquenetta, and Jaquenetta is a true girl; and therefore welcome the sour cup of prosperity! Affliction may one day smile again; and till then, sit thee down, sorrow.

(*Exeunt*)

Scene II

The park

(*Enter* ARMADO *and* MOTH, *his page*)

ARMADO: Boy, what sign is it when a man of great spirit grows melancholy?

MOTH: A great sign, sir, that he will look sad.

ARMADO: Why, sadness is one and the self-same thing, dear imp.

MOTH: No, no; O Lord, sir, no!

ARMADO: How canst thou part sadness and melancholy, my tender juvenal?

MOTH: By a familiar demonstration of the working, my tough signior.

ARMADO: Why tough signior? Why tough signior?

MOTH: Why tender juvenal? Why tender juvenal?

ARMADO: I spoke it, tender juvenal, as a congruent epitheton appertaining to thy young days, which we may nominate tender.

MOTH: And I, tough signior, as an appertinent title to your old time, which we may name tough.

ARMADO: Pretty and apt.

MOTH: How mean you, sir? I pretty, and my saying apt? or I apt, and my saying pretty?

ARMADO: Thou pretty, because little.

MOTH: Little pretty, because little. Wherefore apt?

ARMADO: And therefore apt, because quick.

MOTH: Speak you this in my praise, master?

ARMADO: In thy condign praise.

MOTH: I will praise an eel with the same praise.

ARMADO: That an eel is ingenious?

MOTH: That an eel is quick.

ARMADO: I do say thou art quick in answers; thou heat'st my blood.

MOTH: I am answer'd, sir.

ARMADO: I love not to be cross'd.

MOTH: (*Aside*) He speaks the mere contrary: crosses love not him.

ARMADO: I have promised to study three years with the Duke.

MOTH: You may do it in an hour, sir.

ARMADO: Impossible.

MOTH: How many is one thrice told?

ARMADO: I am ill at reck'ning; it fitteth the spirit of a tapster.

MOTH: You are a gentleman and a gamester, sir.

ARMADO: I confess both; they are both the varnish of a complete man.

MOTH: Then I am sure you know how much the gross sum of deuce-ace amounts to.

ARMADO: It doth amount to one more than two.

MOTH: Which the base vulgar do call three.

ARMADO: True.

MOTH: Why, sir, is this such a piece of study? Now here is three studied ere ye'll thrice wink; and how easy it is to put "years" to the word "three," and study three years in two words, the dancing horse will tell you.

ARMADO: A most fine figure!

MOTH: (*Aside*) To prove you a cipher.

ARMADO: I will hereupon confess I am in love. And as it is base for a soldier to love, so am I in love with a base wench. If drawing my sword against the humour of affection would deliver me from the reprobate thought of it, I would take Desire prisoner, and ransom him to any French courtier for a new-devis'd curtsy. I think scorn to sigh; methinks I should out-swear Cupid.
Comfort me, boy; what great men have been in love?

MOTH: Hercules, master.

ARMADO: Most sweet Hercules! More authority, dear boy, name more; and, sweet my child, let them be men of good repute and carriage.

MOTH: Samson, master; he was a man of good carriage, great carriage, for he carried the town gates on his back like a porter; and he was in love.

ARMADO: O well-knit Samson! strong-jointed Samson! I do excel thee in my rapier as much as thou didst me in carrying gates. I am in love too. Who was Samson's love, my dear Moth?

MOTH: A woman, master.

ARMADO: Of what complexion?

MOTH: Of all the four, or the three, or the two, or one of the four.

ARMADO: Tell me precisely of what complexion.

MOTH: Of the sea-water green, sir.

ARMADO: Is that one of the four complexions?

MOTH: As I have read, sir; and the best of them too.

ARMADO: Green, indeed, is the colour of lovers; but to have a love of that colour, methinks Samson had small reason for it. He surely affected her for her wit.

MOTH: It was so, sir; for she had a green wit.

ARMADO: My love is most immaculate white and red.

MOTH: Most maculate thoughts, master, are mask'd under such colours.

ARMADO: Define, define, well-educated infant.

MOTH: My father's wit my mother's tongue assist me!

ARMADO: Sweet invocation of a child; most pretty, and pathetical!

MOTH: If she be made of white and red,
    Her faults will ne'er be known;
For blushing cheeks by faults are bred,
    And fears by pale white shown.
Then if she fear, or be to blame,
    By this you shall not know;
For still her cheeks possess the same
    Which native she doth owe.
    A dangerous rhyme, master, against the reason of white and red.

ARMADO: Is there not a ballad, boy, of the King and the Beggar?

MOTH: The world was very guilty of such a ballad some three ages since; but I think now 'tis not to be found; or if it were, it would neither serve for the writing nor the tune.

ARMADO: I will have that subject newly writ o'er, that I may example my digression by some mighty precedent. Boy, I do love that country girl that I took in the park with the rational hind Costard; she deserves well.

MOTH: (*Aside*) To be whipt; and yet a better love than my master.

ARMADO: Sing, boy; my spirit grows heavy in love.

MOTH: And that's great marvel, loving a light wench.

ARMADO: I say, sing.

MOTH: Forbear till this company be past.

Enter DULL, COSTARD, *and* JAQUENETTA

DULL: Sir, the Duke's pleasure is that you keep Costard safe; and you must suffer him to take no delight nor no penance; but 'a must fast three days a week. For this damsel, I must keep her at the park; she is allow'd for the day-woman. Fare you well.

ARMADO: I do betray myself with blushing. Maid!

JAQUENETTA: Man!

ARMADO: I will visit thee at the lodge.

JAQUENETTA: That's hereby.

ARMADO: I know where it is situate.

JAQUENETTA: Lord, how wise you are!

ARMADO: I will tell thee wonders.

JAQUENETTA: With that face?

ARMADO: I love thee.

JAQUENETTA: So I heard you say.

ARMADO: And so, farewell.

JAQUENETTA: Fair weather after you!

DULL: Come, Jaquenetta, away.

Exit with JAQUENETTA

ARMADO: Villain, thou shalt fast for thy offences ere thou be pardoned.

COSTARD: Well, sir, I hope when I do it I shall do it on a full stomach.

ARMADO: Thou shalt be heavily punished.

COSTARD: I am more bound to you than your fellows, for they are but lightly rewarded.

ARMADO: Take away this villain; shut him up.

MOTH: Come, you transgressing slave, away.

COSTARD: Let me not be pent up, sir; I will fast, being loose.

MOTH: No, sir; that were fast, and loose. Thou shalt to prison.

COSTARD: Well, if ever I do see the merry days of desolation that I have seen, some shall see.

MOTH: What shall some see?

COSTARD: Nay, nothing, Master Moth, but what they look upon. It is not for prisoners to be too silent in their words, and therefore I will say nothing. I thank God I have as little patience as another man, and therefore I can be quiet.

Exeunt MOTH *and* COSTARD

ARMADO: I do affect the very ground, which is base, where her shoe, which is baser, guided by her foot, which is basest, doth tread. I shall be forsworn—which is a great argument of falsehood—if I love. And how can that be true love which is falsely attempted? Love is a familiar; Love is a devil. There is no evil angel but Love. Yet was Samson so tempted, and he had an excellent strength; yet was Solomon so seduced, and he had a very good wit. Cupid's butt-shaft is too hard for Hercules' club, and therefore too much odds for a Spaniard's rapier. The first and second cause will not serve my turn; the passado he respects not, the duello he regards not; his disgrace is to be called boy, but his glory is to subdue men. Adieu, valour; rust, rapier; be still, drum; for your manager is in love; yea, he loveth. Assist me, some extemporal god of rhyme, for I am sure I shall turn sonnet. Devise, wit; write, pen; for I am for whole volumes in folio.

Exit

ACT II

Scene I

The park

Enter the PRINCESS OF FRANCE, *with three attending ladies,* ROSALINE, MARIA, KATHARINE, BOYET, *and two other* LORDS

BOYET: Now, madam, summon up your dearest spirits.
    Consider who the King your father sends,
    To whom he sends, and what's his embassy:
    Yourself, held precious in the world's esteem,
    To parley with the sole inheritor
    Of all perfections that a man may owe,
    Matchless Navarre; the plea of no less weight
    Than Aquitaine, a dowry for a queen.
    Be now as prodigal of all dear grace
    As Nature was in making graces dear,
    When she did starve the general world beside
    And prodigally gave them all to you.
PRINCESS OF FRANCE: Good Lord Boyet, my beauty, though but mean,
    Needs not the painted flourish of your praise.
    Beauty is bought by judgment of the eye,
    Not utt'red by base sale of chapmen's tongues;
    I am less proud to hear you tell my worth
    Than you much willing to be counted wise
    In spending your wit in the praise of mine.
    But now to task the tasker: good Boyet,
    You are not ignorant all-telling fame
    Doth noise abroad Navarre hath made a vow,
    Till painful study shall outwear three years,
    No woman may approach his silent court.
    Therefore to's seemeth it a needful course,
    Before we enter his forbidden gates,
    To know his pleasure; and in that behalf,
    Bold of your worthiness, we single you
    As our best-moving fair solicitor.
    Tell him the daughter of the King of France,
    On serious business, craving quick dispatch,

Importunes personal conference with his Grace.
Haste, signify so much; while we attend,
Like humble-visag'd suitors, his high will.
BOYET: Proud of employment, willingly I go.
PRINCESS OF FRANCE: All pride is willing pride, and yours is so.

(Exit BOYET)

Who are the votaries, my loving lords,
That are vow-fellows with this virtuous duke?
FIRST LORD: Lord Longaville is one.
PRINCESS OF FRANCE: Know you the man?
MARIA: I know him, madam; at a marriage feast,
Between Lord Perigort and the beauteous heir
Of Jaques Falconbridge, solemnized
In Normandy, saw I this Longaville.
A man of sovereign parts, peerless esteem'd,
Well fitted in arts, glorious in arms;
Nothing becomes him ill that he would well.
The only soil of his fair virtue's gloss,
If virtue's gloss will stain with any soil,
Is a sharp wit match'd with too blunt a will,
Whose edge hath power to cut, whose will still wills
It should none spare that come within his power.
PRINCESS OF FRANCE: Some merry mocking lord, belike; is't so?
MARIA: They say so most that most his humours know.
PRINCESS OF FRANCE: Such short-liv'd wits do wither as they grow.
Who are the rest?
KATHARINE: The young Dumain, a well-accomplish'd youth,
Of all that virtue love for virtue loved;
Most power to do most harm, least knowing ill,
For he hath wit to make an ill shape good,
And shape to win grace though he had no wit.
I saw him at the Duke Alencon's once;
And much too little of that good I saw
Is my report to his great worthiness.
ROSALINE: Another of these students at that time
Was there with him, if I have heard a truth.
Berowne they call him; but a merrier man,
Within the limit of becoming mirth,
I never spent an hour's talk withal.

His eye begets occasion for his wit,
For every object that the one doth catch
The other turns to a mirth-moving jest,
Which his fair tongue, conceit's expositor,
Delivers in such apt and gracious words
That aged ears play truant at his tales,
And younger hearings are quite ravished;
So sweet and voluble is his discourse.

PRINCESS OF FRANCE: God bless my ladies! Are they all in love,
That everyone her own hath garnished
With such bedecking ornaments of praise?

FIRST LORD: Here comes Boyet.

Re-enter BOYET

PRINCESS OF FRANCE: Now, what admittance, lord?

BOYET: Navarre had notice of your fair approach,
And he and his competitors in oath
Were all address'd to meet you, gentle lady,
Before I came. Marry, thus much I have learnt:
He rather means to lodge you in the field,
Like one that comes here to besiege his court,
Than seek a dispensation for his oath,
To let you enter his unpeopled house.

(*The* LADIES-IN-WAITING *mask*)

Enter KING, LONGAVILLE, DUMAIN, BEROWNE, *and* ATTENDANTS
Here comes Navarre.

KING: Fair Princess, welcome to the court of Navarre.

PRINCESS OF FRANCE: "Fair" I give you back again; and "welcome"
I have not yet. The roof of this court is too high to be yours, and
welcome to the wide fields too base to be mine.

KING: You shall be welcome, madam, to my court.

PRINCESS OF FRANCE: I will be welcome then; conduct me thither.

KING: Hear me, dear lady: I have sworn an oath—

PRINCESS OF FRANCE: Our Lady help my lord! He'll be forsworn.

KING: Not for the world, fair madam, by my will.

PRINCESS OF FRANCE: Why, will shall break it; will, and nothing else.

KING: Your ladyship is ignorant what it is.

PRINCESS OF FRANCE: Were my lord so, his ignorance were wise,
Where now his knowledge must prove ignorance.
I hear your Grace hath sworn out house-keeping.

'Tis deadly sin to keep that oath, my lord,
And sin to break it.
But pardon me, I am too sudden bold;
To teach a teacher ill beseemeth me.
Vouchsafe to read the purpose of my coming,
And suddenly resolve me in my suit.

(Giving a paper)

KING: Madam, I will, if suddenly I may.

PRINCESS OF FRANCE: You will the sooner that I were away,
For you'll prove perjur'd if you make me stay.

BEROWNE: Did not I dance with you in Brabant once?

KATHARINE: Did not I dance with you in Brabant once?

BEROWNE: I know you did.

KATHARINE: How needless was it then to ask the question!

BEROWNE: You must not be so quick.

KATHARINE: 'Tis long of you, that spur me with such questions.

BEROWNE: Your wit's too hot, it speeds too fast, 'twill tire.

KATHARINE: Not till it leave the rider in the mire.

BEROWNE: What time o' day?

KATHARINE: The hour that fools should ask.

BEROWNE: Now fair befall your mask!

KATHARINE: Fair fall the face it covers!

BEROWNE: And send you many lovers!

KATHARINE: Amen, so you be none.

BEROWNE: Nay, then will I be gone.

KING: Madam, your father here doth intimate
The payment of a hundred thousand crowns;
Being but the one half of an entire sum
Disbursed by my father in his wars.
But say that he or we, as neither have,
Receiv'd that sum, yet there remains unpaid
A hundred thousand more, in surety of the which,
One part of Aquitaine is bound to us,
Although not valued to the money's worth.
If then the King your father will restore
But that one half which is unsatisfied,
We will give up our right in Aquitaine,
And hold fair friendship with his Majesty.
But that, it seems, he little purposeth,

For here he doth demand to have repaid
A hundred thousand crowns; and not demands,
On payment of a hundred thousand crowns,
To have his title live in Aquitaine;
Which we much rather had depart withal,
And have the money by our father lent,
Than Aquitaine so gelded as it is.
Dear Princess, were not his requests so far
From reason's yielding, your fair self should make
A yielding 'gainst some reason in my breast,
And go well satisfied to France again.

PRINCESS OF FRANCE: You do the King my father too much wrong,
And wrong the reputation of your name,
In so unseeming to confess receipt
Of that which hath so faithfully been paid.

KING: I do protest I never heard of it;
And, if you prove it, I'll repay it back
Or yield up Aquitaine.

PRINCESS OF FRANCE: We arrest your word.
Boyet, you can produce acquittances
For such a sum from special officers
Of Charles his father.

KING: Satisfy me so.

BOYET: So please your Grace, the packet is not come,
Where that and other specialties are bound;
Tomorrow you shall have a sight of them.

KING: It shall suffice me; at which interview
All liberal reason I will yield unto.
Meantime receive such welcome at my hand
As honour, without breach of honour, may
Make tender of to thy true worthiness.
You may not come, fair Princess, within my gates;
But here without you shall be so receiv'd
As you shall deem yourself lodg'd in my heart,
Though so denied fair harbour in my house.
Your own good thoughts excuse me, and farewell.
Tomorrow shall we visit you again.

PRINCESS OF FRANCE: Sweet health and fair desires consort your
Grace!

KING: Thy own wish wish I thee in every place.

(Exit with attendants)

BEROWNE: Lady, I will commend you to mine own heart.

ROSALINE: Pray you, do my commendations;
    I would be glad to see it.

BEROWNE: I would you heard it groan.

ROSALINE: Is the fool sick?

BEROWNE: Sick at the heart.

ROSALINE: Alack, let it blood.

BEROWNE: Would that do it good?

ROSALINE: My physic says "ay."

BEROWNE: Will You prick't with your eye?

ROSALINE: No point, with my knife.

BEROWNE: Now, God save thy life!

ROSALINE: And yours from long living!

BEROWNE: I cannot stay thanksgiving.

(Retiring)

DUMAIN: Sir, I pray you, a word: what lady is that same?

BOYET: The heir of Alencon, Katharine her name.

DUMAIN: A gallant lady! Monsieur, fare you well.

Exit

LONGAVILLE: I beseech you a word: what is she in the white?

BOYET: A woman sometimes, an you saw her in the light.

LONGAVILLE: Perchance light in the light. I desire her name.

BOYET: She hath but one for herself; to desire that were a shame.

LONGAVILLE: Pray you, sir, whose daughter?

BOYET: Her mother's, I have heard.

LONGAVILLE: God's blessing on your beard!

BOYET: Good sir, be not offended;
    She is an heir of Falconbridge.

LONGAVILLE: Nay, my choler is ended.
    She is a most sweet lady.

BOYET: Not unlike, sir; that may be.

Exit LONGAVILLE

BEROWNE: What's her name in the cap?

BOYET: Rosaline, by good hap.

BEROWNE: Is she wedded or no?

BOYET: To her will, sir, or so.

BEROWNE: You are welcome, sir; adieu!

BOYET: Farewell to me, sir, and welcome to you.

Exit BEROWNE. LADIES *Unmask*

MARIA: That last is Berowne, the merry mad-cap lord;

Not a word with him but a jest.

BOYET: And every jest but a word.

PRINCESS OF FRANCE: It was well done of you to take him at his word.

BOYET: I was as willing to grapple as he was to board.

KATHARINE: Two hot sheeps, marry!

BOYET: And wherefore not ships?

No sheep, sweet lamb, unless we feed on your lips.

KATHARINE: You sheep and I pasture—shall that finish the jest?

BOYET: So you grant pasture for me.

(Offering to kiss her)

KATHARINE: Not so, gentle beast;

My lips are no common, though several they be.

BOYET: Belonging to whom?

KATHARINE: To my fortunes and me.

PRINCESS OF FRANCE: Good wits will be jangling; but, gentles, agree;

This civil war of wits were much better used

On Navarre and his book-men, for here 'tis abused.

BOYET: If my observation, which very seldom lies,

By the heart's still rhetoric disclosed with eyes,

Deceive me not now, Navarre is infected.

PRINCESS OF FRANCE: With what?

BOYET: With that which we lovers entitle "affected."

PRINCESS OF FRANCE: Your reason?

BOYET: Why, all his behaviours did make their retire

To the court of his eye, peeping thorough desire.

His heart, like an agate, with your print impressed,

Proud with his form, in his eye pride expressed;

His tongue, all impatient to speak and not see,

Did stumble with haste in his eyesight to be;

All senses to that sense did make their repair,

To feel only looking on fairest of fair.

Methought all his senses were lock'd in his eye,

As jewels in crystal for some prince to buy;

Who, tend'ring their own worth from where they were glass'd,

Did point you to buy them, along as you pass'd.

His face's own margent did quote such amazes

That all eyes saw his eyes enchanted with gazes.
I'll give you Aquitaine and all that is his,
An you give him for my sake but one loving kiss.

PRINCESS OF FRANCE: Come, to our pavilion. Boyet is dispos'd.

BOYET: But to speak that in words which his eye hath disclos'd;
I only have made a mouth of his eye,
By adding a tongue which I know will not lie.

MARIA: Thou art an old love-monger, and speakest skilfully.

KATHARINE: He is Cupid's grandfather, and learns news of him.

ROSALINE: Then was Venus like her mother; for her father is but grim.

BOYET: Do you hear, my mad wenches?

MARIA: No.

BOYET: What, then; do you see?

MARIA: Ay, our way to be gone.

BOYET: You are too hard for me.

Exeunt

ACT III

Scene I

The park

Enter Armado *and* Moth

Armado: Warble, child; make passionate my sense of hearing.

(Moth *sings Concolinel*)

Armado: Sweet air! Go, tenderness of years, take this key, give enlargement to the swain, bring him festinately hither; I must employ him in a letter to my love.

Moth: Master, will you win your love with a French brawl?

Armado: How meanest thou? Brawling in French?

Moth: No, my complete master; but to jig off a tune at the tongue's end, canary to it with your feet, humour it with turning up your eyelids, sigh a note and sing a note, sometime through the throat, as if you swallowed love with singing love, sometime through the nose, as if you snuff'd up love by smelling love, with your hat penthouse-like o'er the shop of your eyes, with your arms cross'd on your thin-belly doublet, like a rabbit on a spit, or your hands in your pocket, like a man after the old painting; and keep not too long in one tune, but a snip and away.

These are complements, these are humours; these betray nice wenches, that would be betrayed without these; and make them men of note—do you note me?—that most are affected to these.

Armado: How hast thou purchased this experience?

Moth: By my penny of observation.

Armado: But O—but O—

Moth: The hobby-horse is forgot.

Armado: Call'st thou my love "hobby-horse"?

Moth: No, master; the hobby-horse is but a colt, and your love perhaps a hackney. But have you forgot your love?

Armado: Almost I had.

Moth: Negligent student! learn her by heart.

Armado: By heart and in heart, boy.

Moth: And out of heart, master; all those three I will prove.

Armado: What wilt thou prove?

MOTH: A man, if I live; and this, by, in, and without, upon the instant.
By heart you love her, because your heart cannot come by her; in
heart you love her, because your heart is in love with her; and out
of heart you love her, being out of heart that you cannot enjoy her.

ARMADO: I am all these three.

MOTH: And three times as much more, and yet nothing at all.

ARMADO: Fetch hither the swain; he must carry me a letter.

MOTH: A message well sympathiz'd—a horse to be ambassador for
an ass.

ARMADO: Ha, ha, what sayest thou?

MOTH: Marry, sir, you must send the ass upon the horse, for he is very
slow-gaited. But I go.

ARMADO: The way is but short; away.

MOTH: As swift as lead, sir.

ARMADO: The meaning, pretty ingenious?
Is not lead a metal heavy, dull, and slow?

MOTH: Minime, honest master; or rather, master, no.

ARMADO: I say lead is slow.

MOTH: You are too swift, sir, to say so:
Is that lead slow which is fir'd from a gun?

ARMADO: Sweet smoke of rhetoric!
He reputes me a cannon; and the bullet, that's he;
I shoot thee at the swain.

MOTH: Thump, then, and I flee.

Exit

ARMADO: A most acute juvenal; volable and free of grace!
By thy favour, sweet welkin, I must sigh in thy face;
Most rude melancholy, valour gives thee place.
My herald is return'd.

Re-enter MOTH *with* COSTARD

MOTH: A wonder, master! here's a costard broken in a shin.

ARMADO: Some enigma, some riddle; come, thy l'envoy; begin.

COSTARD: No egma, no riddle, no l'envoy; no salve in the mail, sir.
O, sir, plantain, a plain plantain; no l'envoy, no l'envoy; no salve, sir,
but a plantain!

ARMADO: By virtue thou enforcest laughter; thy silly thought, my
spleen; the heaving of my lungs provokes me to ridiculous smiling.
O, pardon me, my stars! Doth the inconsiderate take salve for
l'envoy, and the word "l'envoy" for a salve?

MOTH: Do the wise think them other? Is not l'envoy a salve?

ARMADO: No, page; it is an epilogue or discourse to make plain
Some obscure precedence that hath tofore been sain.
I will example it:
The fox, the ape, and the humble-bee,
Were still at odds, being but three.
There's the moral. Now the l'envoy.

MOTH: I will add the l'envoy. Say the moral again.

ARMADO: The fox, the ape, and the humble-bee,
Were still at odds, being but three.

MOTH: Until the goose came out of door,
And stay'd the odds by adding four.
Now will I begin your moral, and do you follow with my l'envoy.
The fox, the ape, and the humble-bee,
Were still at odds, being but three.

ARMADO: Until the goose came out of door,
Staying the odds by adding four.

MOTH: A good l'envoy, ending in the goose; would you desire
more?

COSTARD: The boy hath sold him a bargain, a goose, that's flat.
Sir, your pennyworth is good, an your goose be fat.
To sell a bargain well is as cunning as fast and loose;
Let me see: a fat l'envoy; ay, that's a fat goose.

ARMADO: Come hither, come hither. How did this argument begin?

MOTH: By saying that a costard was broken in a shin.
Then call'd you for the l'envoy.

COSTARD: True, and I for a plantain. Thus came your argument in;
Then the boy's fat l'envoy, the goose that you bought;
And he ended the market.

ARMADO: But tell me: how was there a costard broken in a shin?

MOTH: I will tell you sensibly.

COSTARD: Thou hast no feeling of it, Moth; I will speak that l'envoy.
I, Costard, running out, that was safely within,
Fell over the threshold and broke my shin.

ARMADO: We will talk no more of this matter.

COSTARD: Till there be more matter in the shin.

ARMADO: Sirrah Costard. I will enfranchise thee.

COSTARD: O, Marry me to one Frances! I smell some l'envoy, some
goose, in this.

ARMADO: By my sweet soul, I mean setting thee at liberty, enfreedoming thy person; thou wert immured, restrained, captivated, bound.

COSTARD: True, true; and now you will be my purgation, and let me loose.

ARMADO: I give thee thy liberty, set thee from durance; and, in lieu thereof, impose on thee nothing but this: bear this significant (*giving a letter*) to the country maid Jaquenetta; there is remuneration, for the best ward of mine honour is rewarding my dependents. Moth, follow.

Exit

MOTH: Like the sequel, I. Signior Costard, adieu.

COSTARD: My sweet ounce of man's flesh, my incony Jew!

(*Exit* MOTH)

Now will I look to his remuneration. Remuneration! O, that's the Latin word for three farthings. Three farthings—remuneration.

"What's the price of this inkle?"—"One penny."—"No, I'll give you a remuneration." Why, it carries it. Remuneration! Why, it is a fairer name than French crown. I will never buy and sell out of this word.

Enter BEROWNE

BEROWNE: My good knave Costard, exceedingly well met!

COSTARD: Pray you, sir, how much carnation ribbon may a man buy for a remuneration?

BEROWNE: What is a remuneration?

COSTARD: Marry, sir, halfpenny farthing.

BEROWNE: Why, then, three-farthing worth of silk.

COSTARD: I thank your worship. God be wi' you!

BEROWNE: Stay, slave; I must employ thee.

As thou wilt win my favour, good my knave,

Do one thing for me that I shall entreat.

COSTARD: When would you have it done, sir?

BEROWNE: This afternoon.

COSTARD: Well, I will do it, sir; fare you well.

BEROWNE: Thou knowest not what it is.

COSTARD: I shall know, sir, when I have done it.

BEROWNE: Why, villain, thou must know first.

COSTARD: I will come to your worship tomorrow morning.

BEROWNE: It must be done this afternoon.
  Hark, slave, it is but this:
  The Princess comes to hunt here in the park,
  And in her train there is a gentle lady;
  When tongues speak sweetly, then they name her name,
  And Rosaline they call her. Ask for her,
  And to her white hand see thou do commend
  This seal'd-up counsel. There's thy guerdon; go.

(Giving him a shilling)

COSTARD: Gardon, O sweet gardon! better than remuneration; a
  'leven-pence farthing better; most sweet gardon! I will do it, sir, in
  print. Gardon—remuneration!

Exit

BEROWNE: And I, forsooth, in love; I, that have been love's whip;
  A very beadle to a humorous sigh;
  A critic, nay, a night-watch constable;
  A domineering pedant o'er the boy,
  Than whom no mortal so magnificent!
  This wimpled, whining, purblind, wayward boy,
  This senior-junior, giant-dwarf, Dan Cupid;
  Regent of love-rhymes, lord of folded arms,
  Th' anointed sovereign of sighs and groans,
  Liege of all loiterers and malcontents,
  Dread prince of plackets, king of codpieces,
  Sole imperator, and great general
  Of trotting paritors. O my little heart!
  And I to be a corporal of his field,
  And wear his colours like a tumbler's hoop!
  What! I love, I sue, I seek a wife—
  A woman, that is like a German clock,
  Still a-repairing, ever out of frame,
  And never going aright, being a watch,
  But being watch'd that it may still go right!
  Nay, to be perjur'd, which is worst of all;
  And, among three, to love the worst of all,
  A whitely wanton with a velvet brow,
  With two pitch balls stuck in her face for eyes;
  Ay, and, by heaven, one that will do the deed,
  Though Argus were her eunuch and her guard.

And I to sigh for her! to watch for her!
To pray for her! Go to; it is a plague
That Cupid will impose for my neglect
Of his almighty dreadful little might.
Well, I will love, write, sigh, pray, sue, and groan
Some men must love my lady, and some Joan.

Exit

ACT IV

Scene I

The park

Enter the Princess, Rosaline, Maria, Katharine, Boyet, Lords, Attendants, *and a* Forester

Princess of France: Was that the King that spurr'd his horse so hard
 Against the steep uprising of the hill?
Boyet: I know not; but I think it was not he.
Princess of France: Whoe'er 'a was, 'a show'd a mounting mind.
 Well, lords, today we shall have our dispatch;
 On Saturday we will return to France.
 Then, forester, my friend, where is the bush
 That we must stand and play the murderer in?
Forester: Hereby, upon the edge of yonder coppice;
 A stand where you may make the fairest shoot.
Princess of France: I thank my beauty I am fair that shoot,
 And thereupon thou speak'st the fairest shoot.
Forester: Pardon me, madam, for I meant not so.
Princess of France: What, what? First praise me, and again say no?
 O short-liv'd pride! Not fair? Alack for woe!
Forester: Yes, madam, fair.
Princess of France: Nay, never paint me now;
 Where fair is not, praise cannot mend the brow.
 Here, good my glass, take this for telling true:

 (Giving him money)

 Fair payment for foul words is more than due.
Forester: Nothing but fair is that which you inherit.
Princess of France: See, see, my beauty will be sav'd by merit.
 O heresy in fair, fit for these days!
 A giving hand, though foul, shall have fair praise.
 But come, the bow. Now mercy goes to kill,
 And shooting well is then accounted ill;
 Thus will I save my credit in the shoot:
 Not wounding, pity would not let me do't;
 If wounding, then it was to show my skill,

That more for praise than purpose meant to kill.
And, out of question, so it is sometimes:
Glory grows guilty of detested crimes,
When, for fame's sake, for praise, an outward part,
We bend to that the working of the heart;
As I for praise alone now seek to spill
The poor deer's blood that my heart means no ill.

BOYET: Do not curst wives hold that self-sovereignty
Only for praise sake, when they strive to be
Lords o'er their lords?

PRINCESS OF FRANCE: Only for praise; and praise we may afford
To any lady that subdues a lord.

Enter COSTARD

BOYET: Here comes a member of the commonwealth.

COSTARD: God dig-you-den all! Pray you, which is the head lady?

PRINCESS OF FRANCE: Thou shalt know her, fellow, by the rest that
have no heads.

COSTARD: Which is the greatest lady, the highest?

PRINCESS OF FRANCE: The thickest and the tallest.

COSTARD: The thickest and the tallest! It is so; truth is truth.
An your waist, mistress, were as slender as my wit,
One o' these maids' girdles for your waist should be fit.
Are not you the chief woman? You are the thickest here.

PRINCESS OF FRANCE: What's your will, sir? What's your will?

COSTARD: I have a letter from Monsieur Berowne to one
Lady Rosaline.

PRINCESS OF FRANCE: O, thy letter, thy letter! He's a good friend of
mine.
Stand aside, good bearer. Boyet, you can carve.
Break up this capon.

BOYET: I am bound to serve.
This letter is mistook; it importeth none here.
It is writ to Jaquenetta.

PRINCESS OF FRANCE: We will read it, I swear.
Break the neck of the wax, and everyone give ear.

BOYET: (*Reads*) "By heaven, that thou art fair is most infallible; true
that thou art beauteous; truth itself that thou art lovely. More
fairer than fair, beautiful than beauteous, truer than truth itself,
have commiseration on thy heroical vassal. The magnanimous and

most illustrate king Cophetua set eye upon the pernicious and indubitate beggar Zenelophon; and he it was that might rightly say, 'Veni, vidi, vici'; which to annothanize in the vulgar,—O base and obscure vulgar!—videlicet, He came, saw, and overcame. He came, one; saw, two; overcame, three. Who came?—the king. Why did he come?—to see. Why did he see?—to overcome. To whom came he?—to the beggar. What saw he?—the beggar. Who overcame he?—the beggar. The conclusion is victory; on whose side?—the king's. The captive is enrich'd; on whose side?—the beggar's. The catastrophe is a nuptial; on whose side?—the king's. No, on both in one, or one in both. I am the king, for so stands the comparison; thou the beggar, for so witnesseth thy lowliness. Shall I command thy love? I may. Shall I enforce thy love? I could. Shall I entreat thy love? I will. What shalt thou exchange for rags?— robes, for tittles?—titles, for thyself?—me. Thus expecting thy reply, I profane my lips on thy foot, my eyes on thy picture, and my heart on thy every part."

Thine in the dearest design of industry.

DON ADRIANO DE ARMADO: "Thus dost thou hear the Nemean lion roar

'Gainst thee, thou lamb, that standest as his prey;

Submissive fall his princely feet before,

And he from forage will incline to play.

But if thou strive, poor soul, what are thou then?

Food for his rage, repasture for his den."

PRINCESS OF FRANCE: What plume of feathers is he that indited this letter?

What vane? What weathercock? Did you ever hear better?

BOYET: I am much deceived but I remember the style.

PRINCESS OF FRANCE: Else your memory is bad, going o'er it erewhile.

BOYET: This Armado is a Spaniard, that keeps here in court;

A phantasime, a Monarcho, and one that makes sport

To the Prince and his book-mates.

PRINCESS OF FRANCE: Thou fellow, a word.

Who gave thee this letter?

COSTARD: I told you: my lord.

PRINCESS OF FRANCE: To whom shouldst thou give it?

COSTARD: From my lord to my lady.

PRINCESS OF FRANCE: From which lord to which lady?

COSTARD: From my Lord Berowne, a good master of mine,
    To a lady of France that he call'd Rosaline.
PRINCESS OF FRANCE: Thou hast mistaken his letter. Come, lords,
    away.
    (*To* ROSALINE) Here, sweet, put up this; 'twill be thine
    another day.

Exeunt PRINCESS *and* TRAIN

BOYET: Who is the shooter? who is the shooter?
ROSALINE: Shall I teach you to know?
BOYET: Ay, my continent of beauty.
ROSALINE: Why, she that bears the bow.
    Finely put off!
BOYET: My lady goes to kill horns; but, if thou marry,
    Hang me by the neck, if horns that year miscarry.
    Finely put on!
ROSALINE: Well then, I am the shooter.
BOYET: And who is your deer?
ROSALINE: If we choose by the horns, yourself come not near.
    Finely put on indeed!
MARIA: You Still wrangle with her, Boyet, and she strikes at the brow.
BOYET: But she herself is hit lower. Have I hit her now?
ROSALINE: Shall I come upon thee with an old saying, that was a man
    when King Pepin of France was a little boy, as touching the hit it?
BOYET: So I may answer thee with one as old, that was a woman
    when Queen Guinever of Britain was a little wench, as touching
    the hit it.
ROSALINE: (*Singing*)
    Thou canst not hit it, hit it, hit it,
    Thou canst not hit it, my good man.
BOYET: An I cannot, cannot, cannot,
    An I cannot, another can.

Exeunt ROSALINE *and* KATHARINE

COSTARD: By my troth, most pleasant! How both did fit it!
MARIA: A mark marvellous well shot; for they both did hit it.
BOYET: A mark! O, mark but that mark! A mark, says my lady!
    Let the mark have a prick in't, to mete at, if it may be.
MARIA: Wide o' the bow-hand! I' faith, your hand is out.
COSTARD: Indeed, 'a must shoot nearer, or he'll ne'er hit the clout.
BOYET: An if my hand be out, then belike your hand is in.

COSTARD: Then will she get the upshoot by cleaving the pin.
MARIA: Come, come, you talk greasily; your lips grow foul.
COSTARD: She's too hard for you at pricks, sir; challenge her to bowl.
BOYET: I fear too much rubbing; goodnight, my good owl.

Exeunt BOYET *and* MARIA

COSTARD: By my soul, a swain, a most simple clown!
    Lord, Lord! how the ladies and I have put him down!
    O' my troth, most sweet jests, most incony vulgar wit!
    When it comes so smoothly off, so obscenely, as it were, so fit.
    Armado a th' t'one side—O, a most dainty man!
    To see him walk before a lady and to bear her fan!
    To see him kiss his hand, and how most sweetly 'a will swear!
    And his page o' t' other side, that handful of wit!
    Ah, heavens, it is a most pathetical nit!
    Sola, sola!

Exit COSTARD

Scene II

The park

From the shooting within, enter Holofernes, Sir Nathaniel, *and* Dull

Nathaniel: Very reverent sport, truly; and done in the testimony of a good conscience.

Holofernes: The deer was, as you know, sanguis, in blood; ripe as the pomewater, who now hangeth like a jewel in the ear of caelo, the sky, the welkin, the heaven; and anon falleth like a crab on the face of terra, the soil, the land, the earth.

Nathaniel: Truly, Master Holofernes, the epithets are sweetly varied, like a scholar at the least; but, sir, I assure ye it was a buck of the first head.

Holofernes: Sir Nathaniel, haud credo.

Dull: 'Twas not a haud credo; 'twas a pricket.

Holofernes: Most barbarous intimation! yet a kind of insinuation, as it were, in via, in way, of explication; facere, as it were, replication, or rather, ostentare, to show, as it were, his inclination, after his undressed, unpolished, uneducated, unpruned, untrained, or rather unlettered, or ratherest unconfirmed fashion, to insert again my haud credo for a deer.

Dull: I said the deer was not a haud credo; 'twas a pricket.

Holofernes: Twice-sod simplicity, bis coctus!

O thou monster Ignorance, how deformed dost thou look!

Nathaniel: Sir, he hath never fed of the dainties that are bred in a book;

He hath not eat paper, as it were; he hath not drunk ink; his intellect is not replenished; he is only an animal, only sensible in the duller parts;

And such barren plants are set before us that we thankful should be—

Which we of taste and feeling are—for those parts that do fructify in us more than he.

For as it would ill become me to be vain, indiscreet, or a fool,

So, were there a patch set on learning, to see him in a school.

But, omne bene, say I, being of an old father's mind:
Many can brook the weather that love not the wind.

DULL: You two are book-men: can you tell me by your wit
What was a month old at Cain's birth that's not five weeks old as
yet?

HOLOFERNES: Dictynna, goodman Dull; Dictynna, goodman Dull.

DULL: What is Dictynna?

NATHANIEL: A title to Phoebe, to Luna, to the moon.

HOLOFERNES: The moon was a month old when Adam was no more,
And raught not to five weeks when he came to five-score.
Th' allusion holds in the exchange.

DULL: 'Tis true, indeed; the collusion holds in the exchange.

HOLOFERNES: God comfort thy capacity! I say th' allusion holds in the
exchange.

DULL: And I say the polusion holds in the exchange; for the moon is
never but a month old; and I say, beside, that 'twas a pricket that
the Princess kill'd.

HOLOFERNES: Sir Nathaniel, will you hear an extemporal epitaph on
the death of the deer? And, to humour the ignorant, call the deer
the Princess kill'd a pricket.

NATHANIEL: Perge, good Master Holofernes, perge, so it shall please
you to abrogate scurrility.

HOLOFERNES: I will something affect the letter, for it argues
facility.
The preyful Princess pierc'd and prick'd a pretty pleasing pricket.
Some say a sore; but not a sore till now made sore with shooting.
The dogs did yell; put el to sore, then sorel jumps from thicket—
Or pricket sore, or else sorel; the people fall a-hooting.
If sore be sore, then L to sore makes fifty sores o' sorel.
Of one sore I an hundred make by adding but one more L.

NATHANIEL: A rare talent!

DULL: (*Aside*) If a talent be a claw, look how he claws him with a
talent.

HOLOFERNES: This is a gift that I have, simple, simple; a foolish
extravagant spirit, full of forms, figures, shapes, objects, ideas,
apprehensions, motions, revolutions. These are begot in the
ventricle of memory, nourish'd in the womb of pia mater, and
delivered upon the mellowing of occasion. But the gift is good in
those in whom it is acute, and I am thankful for it.

NATHANIEL: Sir, I praise the Lord for you, and so may my parishioners; for their sons are well tutor'd by you, and their daughters profit very greatly under you. You are a good member of the commonwealth.

HOLOFERNES: Mehercle, if their sons be ingenious, they shall want no instruction; if their daughters be capable, I will put it to them; but, vir sapit qui pauca loquitur. A soul feminine saluteth us.

Enter JAQUENETTA *and* COSTARD

JAQUENETTA: God give you good morrow, Master Person.

HOLOFERNES: Master Person, quasi pers-one. And if one should be pierc'd which is the one?

COSTARD: Marry, Master Schoolmaster, he that is likest to a hogshead.

HOLOFERNES: Piercing a hogshead! A good lustre of conceit in a turf of earth; fire enough for a flint, pearl enough for a swine; 'tis pretty; it is well.

JAQUENETTA: Good Master Parson, be so good as read me this letter; it was given me by Costard, and sent me from Don Armado. I beseech you read it.

HOLOFERNES: Fauste, precor gelida quando pecus omne sub umbra Ruminat—and so forth. Ah, good old Mantuan! I may speak of thee as the traveller doth of Venice:

    Venetia, Venetia,

    Chi non ti vede, non ti pretia.

Old Mantuan, old Mantuan! Who understandeth thee not, loves thee not—

    Ut, re, sol, la, mi, fa.

Under pardon, sir, what are the contents? or rather as

Horace says in his—What, my soul, verses?

NATHANIEL: Ay, sir, and very learned.

HOLOFERNES: Let me hear a staff, a stanze, a verse; lege, domine.

NATHANIEL: (*Reads*) "If love make me forsworn, how shall I swear to love?

Ah, never faith could hold, if not to beauty vowed!

Though to myself forsworn, to thee I'll faithful prove;

Those thoughts to me were oaks, to thee like osiers bowed.

Study his bias leaves, and makes his book thine eyes,

Where all those pleasures live that art would comprehend.

If knowledge be the mark, to know thee shall suffice;

Well learned is that tongue that well can thee commend;

All ignorant that soul that sees thee without wonder;
Which is to me some praise that I thy parts admire.
Thy eye Jove's lightning bears, thy voice his dreadful thunder,
Which, not to anger bent, is music and sweet fire.
Celestial as thou art, O, pardon love this wrong,
That singes heaven's praise with such an earthly tongue."

HOLOFERNES: You find not the apostrophas, and so miss the
accent: let me supervise the canzonet. Here are only numbers
ratified; but, for the elegancy, facility, and golden cadence of poesy,
caret. Ovidius Naso was the man. And why, indeed, "Naso" but
for smelling out the odoriferous flowers of fancy, the jerks of
invention? Imitari is nothing: so doth the hound his master, the
ape his keeper, the tired horse his rider. But, damosella virgin, was
this directed to you?

JAQUENETTA: Ay, sir, from one Monsieur Berowne, one of the strange
queen's lords.

HOLOFERNES: I will overglance the superscript: "To the snow-white
hand of the most beauteous Lady Rosaline." I will look again
on the intellect of the letter, for the nomination of the party
writing to the person written unto: "Your Ladyship's in all desired
employment, Berowne." Sir Nathaniel, this Berowne is one of
the votaries with the King; and here he hath framed a letter to a
sequent of the stranger queen's which accidentally, or by the way
of progression, hath miscarried. Trip and go, my sweet; deliver this
paper into the royal hand of the King; it may concern much. Stay
not thy compliment; I forgive thy duty. Adieu.

JAQUENETTA: Good Costard, go with me. Sir, God save your life!

COSTARD: Have with thee, my girl.

Exeunt COSTARD *and* JAQUENETTA

NATHANIEL: Sir, you have done this in the fear of God, very
religiously; and, as a certain father saith—

HOLOFERNES: Sir, tell not me of the father; I do fear colourable
colours. But to return to the verses: did they please you, Sir
Nathaniel?

NATHANIEL: Marvellous well for the pen.

HOLOFERNES: I do dine today at the father's of a certain pupil of
mine; where, if, before repast, it shall please you to gratify the table
with a grace, I will, on my privilege I have with the parents of the
foresaid child or pupil, undertake your ben venuto; where I will

prove those verses to be very unlearned, neither savouring of poetry, wit, nor invention. I beseech your society.

NATHANIEL: And thank you too; for society, saith the text, is the happiness of life.

HOLOFERNES: And certes, the text most infallibly concludes it.

(*To* DULL) Sir, I do invite you too; you shall not say me nay: pauca verba. Away; the gentles are at their game, and we will to our recreation.

Exeunt

Scene III

The park

Enter BEROWNE, *with a paper his hand, alone*

BEROWNE: The King he is hunting the deer: I am coursing myself.
They have pitch'd a toil: I am tolling in a pitch—pitch that defiles.
Defile! a foul word. Well, "set thee down, sorrow!" for so they say
the fool said, and so say I, and I am the fool. Well proved, wit. By
the Lord, this love is as mad as Ajax: it kills sheep; it kills me—I
a sheep. Well proved again o' my side. I will not love; if I do, hang
me. I' faith, I will not. O, but her eye! By this light, but for her eye,
I would not love her—yes, for her two eyes. Well, I do nothing in
the world but lie, and lie in my throat. By heaven, I do love; and it
hath taught me to rhyme, and to be melancholy; and here is part
of my rhyme, and here my melancholy. Well, she hath one o' my
sonnets already; the clown bore it, the fool sent it, and the lady
hath it: sweet clown, sweeter fool, sweetest lady! By the world, I
would not care a pin if the other three were in. Here comes one
with a paper; God give him grace to groan!

(Climbs into a tree)

Enter the KING, *with a paper*

KING: Ay me!

BEROWNE: Shot, by heaven! Proceed, sweet Cupid; thou hast thump'd
him with thy bird-bolt under the left pap. In faith, secrets!

KING: *(Reads)*

"So sweet a kiss the golden sun gives not
To those fresh morning drops upon the rose,
As thy eye-beams, when their fresh rays have smote
The night of dew that on my cheeks down flows;
Nor shines the silver moon one half so bright
Through the transparent bosom of the deep,
As doth thy face through tears of mine give light.
Thou shin'st in every tear that I do weep;
No drop but as a coach doth carry thee;
So ridest thou triumphing in my woe.
Do but behold the tears that swell in me,

And they thy glory through my grief will show.
But do not love thyself; then thou wilt keep
My tears for glasses, and still make me weep.
O queen of queens! how far dost thou excel
No thought can think nor tongue of mortal tell."
How shall she know my griefs? I'll drop the paper—
Sweet leaves, shade folly. Who is he comes here?

(Steps aside)

(Enter LONGAVILLE, *with a paper)*
What, Longaville, and reading! Listen, ear.
BEROWNE: Now, in thy likeness, one more fool appear!
LONGAVILLE: Ay me, I am forsworn!
BEROWNE: Why, he comes in like a perjure, wearing papers.
KING: In love, I hope; sweet fellowship in shame!
BEROWNE: One drunkard loves another of the name.
LONGAVILLE: Am I the first that have been perjur'd so?
BEROWNE: I could put thee in comfort: not by two that I know;
Thou makest the triumviry, the corner-cap of society,
The shape of Love's Tyburn that hangs up simplicity.
LONGAVILLE: I fear these stubborn lines lack power to move.
O sweet Maria, empress of my love!
These numbers will I tear, and write in prose.
BEROWNE: O, rhymes are guards on wanton Cupid's hose:
Disfigure not his slop.
LONGAVILLE: This same shall go.

(He reads the sonnet)

"Did not the heavenly rhetoric of thine eye,
'Gainst whom the world cannot hold argument,
Persuade my heart to this false perjury?
Vows for thee broke deserve not punishment.
A woman I forswore; but I will prove,
Thou being a goddess, I forswore not thee:
My vow was earthly, thou a heavenly love;
Thy grace being gain'd cures all disgrace in me.
Vows are but breath, and breath a vapour is;
Then thou, fair sun, which on my earth dost shine,
Exhal'st this vapour-vow; in thee it is.
If broken, then it is no fault of mine;
If by me broke, what fool is not so wise

To lose an oath to win a paradise?"

BEROWNE: This is the liver-vein, which makes flesh a deity,
    A green goose a goddess—pure, pure idolatry.
    God amend us, God amend! We are much out o' th' way.

Enter DUMAIN, *with a paper*

LONGAVILLE: By whom shall I send this?—Company! Stay.

                                           (*Steps aside*)

BEROWNE: "All hid, all hid"—an old infant play.
    Like a demigod here sit I in the sky,
    And wretched fools' secrets heedfully o'er-eye.
    More sacks to the mill! O heavens, I have my wish!
    Dumain transformed! Four woodcocks in a dish!

DUMAIN: O most divine Kate!

BEROWNE: O most profane coxcomb!

DUMAIN: By heaven, the wonder in a mortal eye!

BEROWNE: By earth, she is not, corporal: there you lie.

DUMAIN: Her amber hairs for foul hath amber quoted.

BEROWNE: An amber-colour'd raven was well noted.

DUMAIN: As upright as the cedar.

BEROWNE: Stoop, I say;
    Her shoulder is with child.

DUMAIN: As fair as day.

BEROWNE: Ay, as some days; but then no sun must shine.

DUMAIN: O that I had my wish!

LONGAVILLE: And I had mine!

KING: And I mine too, good Lord!

BEROWNE: Amen, so I had mine! Is not that a good word?

DUMAIN: I would forget her; but a fever she
    Reigns in my blood, and will rememb'red be.

BEROWNE: A fever in your blood? Why, then incision
    Would let her out in saucers. Sweet misprision!

DUMAIN: Once more I'll read the ode that I have writ.

BEROWNE: Once more I'll mark how love can vary wit.

DUMAIN: (*Reads*)
        "On a day—alack the day!—
        Love, whose month is ever May,
        Spied a blossom passing fair
        Playing in the wanton air.
        Through the velvet leaves the wind,

All unseen, can passage find;
That the lover, sick to death,
Wish'd himself the heaven's breath.
'Air,' quoth he 'thy cheeks may blow;
Air, would I might triumph so!
But, alack, my hand is sworn
Ne'er to pluck thee from thy thorn;
Vow, alack, for youth unmeet,
Youth so apt to pluck a sweet.
Do not call it sin in me
That I am forsworn for thee;
Thou for whom Jove would swear
Juno but an Ethiope were;
And deny himself for Jove,
Turning mortal for thy love.'"
This will I send; and something else more plain
That shall express my true love's fasting pain.
O, would the King, Berowne and Longaville,
Were lovers too! Ill, to example ill,
Would from my forehead wipe a perjur'd note;
For none offend where all alike do dote.

LONGAVILLE: (*Advancing*) Dumain, thy love is far from charity,
That in love's grief desir'st society;
You may look pale, but I should blush, I know,
To be o'erheard and taken napping so.

KING: (*Advancing*) Come, sir, you blush; as his, your case is such.
You chide at him, offending twice as much:
You do not love Maria! Longaville
Did never sonnet for her sake compile;
Nor never lay his wreathed arms athwart
His loving bosom, to keep down his heart.
I have been closely shrouded in this bush,
And mark'd you both, and for you both did blush.
I heard your guilty rhymes, observ'd your fashion,
Saw sighs reek from you, noted well your passion.
"Ay me!" says one. "O Jove!" the other cries.
One, her hairs were gold; crystal the other's eyes.
(*To* LONGAVILLE) You would for paradise break faith and troth;
(*To* DUMAIN) And Jove for your love would infringe an oath.

What will Berowne say when that he shall hear
Faith infringed which such zeal did swear?
How will he scorn, how will he spend his wit!
How will he triumph, leap, and laugh at it!
For all the wealth that ever I did see,
I would not have him know so much by me.
BEROWNE: (*Descending*) Now step I forth to whip hypocrisy,
    Ah, good my liege, I pray thee pardon me.
    Good heart, what grace hast thou thus to reprove
    These worms for loving, that art most in love?
    Your eyes do make no coaches; in your tears
    There is no certain princess that appears;
    You'll not be perjur'd; 'tis a hateful thing;
    Tush, none but minstrels like of sonneting.
    But are you not ashamed? Nay, are you not,
    All three of you, to be thus much o'ershot?
    You found his mote; the King your mote did see;
    But I a beam do find in each of three.
    O, what a scene of fool'ry have I seen,
    Of sighs, of groans, of sorrow, and of teen!
    O, me, with what strict patience have I sat,
    To see a king transformed to a gnat!
    To see great Hercules whipping a gig,
    And profound Solomon to tune a jig,
    And Nestor play at push-pin with the boys,
    And critic Timon laugh at idle toys!
    Where lies thy grief, O, tell me, good Dumain?
    And, gentle Longaville, where lies thy pain?
    And where my liege's? All about the breast.
    A caudle, ho!
KING: Too bitter is thy jest.
    Are we betrayed thus to thy over-view?
BEROWNE: Not you by me, but I betrayed to you.
    I that am honest, I that hold it sin
    To break the vow I am engaged in;
    I am betrayed by keeping company
    With men like you, men of inconstancy.
    When shall you see me write a thing in rhyme?
    Or groan for Joan? or spend a minute's time

In pruning me? When shall you hear that I
Will praise a hand, a foot, a face, an eye,
A gait, a state, a brow, a breast, a waist,
A leg, a limb—

KING: Soft! whither away so fast?
A true man or a thief that gallops so?

BEROWNE: I post from love; good lover, let me go.

Enter JAQUENETTA *and* COSTARD

JAQUENETTA: God bless the King!

KING: What present hast thou there?

COSTARD: Some certain treason.

KING: What makes treason here?

COSTARD: Nay, it makes nothing, sir.

KING: If it mar nothing neither,
The treason and you go in peace away together.

JAQUENETTA: I beseech your Grace, let this letter be read;
Our person misdoubts it: 'twas treason, he said.

KING: Berowne, read it over.

(BEROWNE *reads the letter*)

Where hadst thou it?

JAQUENETTA: Of Costard.

KING: Where hadst thou it?

COSTARD: Of Dun Adramadio, Dun Adramadio.

(BEROWNE *tears the letter*)

KING: How now! What is in you? Why dost thou tear it?

BEROWNE: A toy, my liege, a toy! Your Grace needs not fear it.

LONGAVILLE: It did move him to passion, and therefore let's hear it.

DUMAIN: It is Berowne's writing, and here is his name.

(*Gathering up the pieces*)

BEROWNE: (*To* COSTARD) Ah, you whoreson loggerhead, you were
born to do me shame.

Guilty, my lord, guilty! I confess, I confess.

KING: What?

BEROWNE: That you three fools lack'd me fool to make up the mess;
He, he, and you—and you, my liege!—and I
Are pick-purses in love, and we deserve to die.
O, dismiss this audience, and I shall tell you more.

DUMAIN: Now the number is even.

BEROWNE: True, true, we are four.

Will these turtles be gone?

KING: Hence, sirs, away.

COSTARD: Walk aside the true folk, and let the traitors stay.

(*Exeunt* COSTARD *and* JAQUENETTA)

BEROWNE: Sweet lords, sweet lovers, O, let us embrace!
　　As true we are as flesh and blood can be.
　　The sea will ebb and flow, heaven show his face;
　　Young blood doth not obey an old decree.
　　We cannot cross the cause why we were born,
　　Therefore of all hands must we be forsworn.

KING: What, did these rent lines show some love of thine?

BEROWNE: "Did they?" quoth you. Who sees the heavenly Rosaline
　　That, like a rude and savage man of Inde
　　At the first op'ning of the gorgeous east,
　　Bows not his vassal head and, strucken blind,
　　Kisses the base ground with obedient breast?
　　What peremptory eagle-sighted eye
　　Dares look upon the heaven of her brow
　　That is not blinded by her majesty?

KING: What zeal, what fury hath inspir'd thee now?
　　My love, her mistress, is a gracious moon;
　　She, an attending star, scarce seen a light.

BEROWNE: My eyes are then no eyes, nor I Berowne.
　　O, but for my love, day would turn tonight!
　　Of all complexions the cull'd sovereignty
　　Do meet, as at a fair, in her fair cheek,
　　Where several worthies make one dignity,
　　Where nothing wants that want itself doth seek.
　　Lend me the flourish of all gentle tongues—
　　Fie, painted rhetoric! O, she needs it not!
　　To things of sale a seller's praise belongs:
　　She passes praise; then praise too short doth blot.
　　A wither'd hermit, five-score winters worn,
　　Might shake off fifty, looking in her eye.
　　Beauty doth varnish age, as if new-born,
　　And gives the crutch the cradle's infancy.
　　O, 'tis the sun that maketh all things shine!

KING: By heaven, thy love is black as ebony.

BEROWNE: Is ebony like her? O wood divine!

A wife of such wood were felicity.
O, who can give an oath? Where is a book?
That I may swear beauty doth beauty lack,
If that she learn not of her eye to look.
No face is fair that is not full so black.

KING: O paradox! Black is the badge of hell,
The hue of dungeons, and the school of night;
And beauty's crest becomes the heavens well.

BEROWNE: Devils soonest tempt, resembling spirits of light.
O, if in black my lady's brows be deckt,
It mourns that painting and usurping hair
Should ravish doters with a false aspect;
And therefore is she born to make black fair.
Her favour turns the fashion of the days;
For native blood is counted painting now;
And therefore red that would avoid dispraise
Paints itself black, to imitate her brow.

DUMAIN: To look like her are chimney-sweepers black.

LONGAVILLE: And since her time are colliers counted bright.

KING: And Ethiopes of their sweet complexion crack.

DUMAIN: Dark needs no candles now, for dark is light.

BEROWNE: Your mistresses dare never come in rain
For fear their colours should be wash'd away.

KING: 'Twere good yours did; for, sir, to tell you plain,
I'll find a fairer face not wash'd today.

BEROWNE: I'll prove her fair, or talk till doomsday here.

KING: No devil will fright thee then so much as she.

DUMAIN: I never knew man hold vile stuff so dear.

LONGAVILLE: Look, here's thy love: my foot and her face see.

(Showing his shoe)

BEROWNE: O, if the streets were paved with thine eyes,
Her feet were much too dainty for such tread!

DUMAIN: O vile! Then, as she goes, what upward lies
The street should see as she walk'd overhead.

KING: But what of this? Are we not all in love?

BEROWNE: Nothing so sure; and thereby all forsworn.

KING: Then leave this chat; and, good Berowne, now prove
Our loving lawful, and our faith not torn.

DUMAIN: Ay, marry, there; some flattery for this evil.

LONGAVILLE: O, some authority how to proceed;
    Some tricks, some quillets, how to cheat the devil!
DUMAIN: Some salve for perjury.
BEROWNE: 'Tis more than need.
    Have at you, then, affection's men-at-arms.
    Consider what you first did swear unto:
    To fast, to study, and to see no woman—
    Flat treason 'gainst the kingly state of youth.
    Say, can you fast? Your stomachs are too young,
    And abstinence engenders maladies.
    And, where that you you have vow'd to study, lords,
    In that each of you have forsworn his book,
    Can you still dream, and pore, and thereon look?
    For when would you, my lord, or you, or you,
    Have found the ground of study's excellence
    Without the beauty of a woman's face?
    From women's eyes this doctrine I derive:
    They are the ground, the books, the academes,
    From whence doth spring the true Promethean fire.
    Why, universal plodding poisons up
    The nimble spirits in the arteries,
    As motion and long-during action tires
    The sinewy vigour of the traveller.
    Now, for not looking on a woman's face,
    You have in that forsworn the use of eyes,
    And study too, the causer of your vow;
    For where is author in the world
    Teaches such beauty as a woman's eye?
    Learning is but an adjunct to ourself,
    And where we are our learning likewise is;
    Then when ourselves we see in ladies' eyes,
    With ourselves.
    Do we not likewise see our learning there?
    O, we have made a vow to study, lords,
    And in that vow we have forsworn our books.
    For when would you, my liege, or you, or you,
    In leaden contemplation have found out
    Such fiery numbers as the prompting eyes
    Of beauty's tutors have enrich'd you with?

Other slow arts entirely keep the brain;
And therefore, finding barren practisers,
Scarce show a harvest of their heavy toil;
But love, first learned in a lady's eyes,
Lives not alone immured in the brain,
But with the motion of all elements
Courses as swift as thought in every power,
And gives to every power a double power,
Above their functions and their offices.
It adds a precious seeing to the eye:
A lover's eyes will gaze an eagle blind.
A lover's ear will hear the lowest sound,
When the suspicious head of theft is stopp'd.
Love's feeling is more soft and sensible
Than are the tender horns of cockled snails:
Love's tongue proves dainty Bacchus gross in taste.
For valour, is not Love a Hercules,
Still climbing trees in the Hesperides?
Subtle as Sphinx; as sweet and musical
As bright Apollo's lute, strung with his hair.
And when Love speaks, the voice of all the gods
Make heaven drowsy with the harmony.
Never durst poet touch a pen to write
Until his ink were temp'red with Love's sighs;
O, then his lines would ravish savage ears,
And plant in tyrants mild humility.
From women's eyes this doctrine I derive.
They sparkle still the right Promethean fire;
They are the books, the arts, the academes,
That show, contain, and nourish, all the world,
Else none at all in aught proves excellent.
Then fools you were these women to forswear;
Or, keeping what is sworn, you will prove fools.
For wisdom's sake, a word that all men love;
Or for Love's sake, a word that loves all men;
Or for men's sake, the authors of these women;
Or women's sake, by whom we men are men—
Let us once lose our oaths to find ourselves,
Or else we lose ourselves to keep our oaths.

It is religion to be thus forsworn;
For charity itself fulfils the law,
And who can sever love from charity?

KING: Saint Cupid, then! and, soldiers, to the field!

BEROWNE: Advance your standards, and upon them, lords;
Pell-mell, down with them! be first advis'd,
In conflict, that you get the sun of them.

LONGAVILLE: Now to plain-dealing; lay these glozes by.
Shall we resolve to woo these girls of France?

KING: And win them too; therefore let us devise
Some entertainment for them in their tents.

BEROWNE: First, from the park let us conduct them thither;
Then homeward every man attach the hand
Of his fair mistress. In the afternoon
We will with some strange pastime solace them,
Such as the shortness of the time can shape;
For revels, dances, masks, and merry hours,
Forerun fair Love, strewing her way with flowers.

KING: Away, away! No time shall be omitted
That will betime, and may by us be fitted.

BEROWNE: Allons! allons! Sow'd cockle reap'd no corn,
And justice always whirls in equal measure.
Light wenches may prove plagues to men forsworn;
If so, our copper buys no better treasure.

Exeunt

ACT V

Scene I

The park

Enter HOLOFERNES, SIR NATHANIEL, *and* DULL

HOLOFERNES: Satis quod sufficit.

NATHANIEL: I praise God for you, sir. Your reasons at dinner have been sharp and sententious; pleasant without scurrility, witty without affection, audacious without impudency, learned without opinion, and strange without heresy. I did converse this quondam day with a companion of the King's who is intituled, nominated, or called, Don Adriano de Armado.

HOLOFERNES: Novi hominem tanquam te. His humour is lofty, his discourse peremptory, his tongue filed, his eye ambitious, his gait majestical and his general behaviour vain, ridiculous, and thrasonical. He is too picked, too spruce, too affected, too odd, as it were, too peregrinate, as I may call it.

NATHANIEL: A most singular and choice epithet.

(Draws out his table-book)

HOLOFERNES: He draweth out the thread of his verbosity finer than the staple of his argument. I abhor such fanatical phantasimes, such insociable and point-devise companions; such rackers of orthography, as to speak "dout" fine, when he should say "doubt"; "det" when he should pronounce "debt"—d, e, b, t, not d, e, t.

He clepeth a calf "cauf," half "hauf"; neighbour vocatur "nebour"; "neigh" abbreviated "ne." This is abhominable—which he would call "abbominable." It insinuateth me of insanie: ne intelligis, domine? to make frantic, lunatic.

NATHANIEL: Laus Deo, bone intelligo.

HOLOFERNES: "Bone"?—"bone" for "bene." Priscian a little scratch'd; 'twill serve.

Enter ARMADO, MOTH, *and* COSTARD

NATHANIEL: Videsne quis venit?

HOLOFERNES: Video, et gaudeo.

ARMADO: *(To* MOTH*)* Chirrah!

HOLOFERNES: Quare "chirrah," not "sirrah"?

ARMADO: Men of peace, well encount'red.

HOLOFERNES: Most military sir, salutation.

MOTH: (*Aside to* COSTARD) They have been at a great feast of languages and stol'n the scraps.

COSTARD: O, they have liv'd long on the alms-basket of words. I marvel thy master hath not eaten thee for a word, for thou are not so long by the head as *honorificabilitudinitatibus*; thou art easier swallowed than a flap-dragon.

MOTH: Peace! the peal begins.

ARMADO: (*To* HOLOFERNES) Monsieur, are you not lett'red?

MOTH: Yes, yes; he teaches boys the hornbook. What is a, b, spelt backward with the horn on his head?

HOLOFERNES: Ba, pueritia, with a horn added.

MOTH: Ba, most silly sheep with a horn. You hear his learning.

HOLOFERNES: Quis, quis, thou consonant?

MOTH: The third of the five vowels, if You repeat them; or the fifth, if I.

HOLOFERNES: I will repeat them: a, e, i—

MOTH: The sheep; the other two concludes it: o, u.

ARMADO: Now, by the salt wave of the Mediterraneum, a sweet touch, a quick venue of wit-snip, snap, quick and home. It rejoiceth my intellect. True wit!

MOTH: Offer'd by a child to an old man; which is wit-old.

HOLOFERNES: What is the figure? What is the figure?

MOTH: Horns.

HOLOFERNES: Thou disputes like an infant; go whip thy gig.

MOTH: Lend me your horn to make one, and I will whip about your infamy circum circa—a gig of a cuckold's horn.

COSTARD: An I had but one penny in the world, thou shouldst have it to buy ginger-bread. Hold, there is the very remuneration I had of thy master, thou halfpenny purse of wit, thou pigeon-egg of discretion. O, an the heavens were so pleased that thou wert but my bastard, what a joyful father wouldst thou make me! Go to; thou hast it ad dunghill, at the fingers' ends, as they say.

HOLOFERNES: O, I smell false Latin; "dunghill" for unguem.

ARMADO: Arts-man, preambulate; we will be singuled from the barbarous. Do you not educate youth at the charge-house on the top of the mountain?

HOLOFERNES: Or mons, the hill.

ARMADO: At your sweet pleasure, for the mountain.

HOLOFERNES: I do, sans question.

ARMADO: Sir, it is the King's most sweet pleasure and affection to congratulate the Princess at her pavilion, in the posteriors of this day; which the rude multitude call the afternoon.

HOLOFERNES: The posterior of the day, most generous sir, is liable, congruent, and measurable, for the afternoon. The word is well cull'd, chose, sweet, and apt, I do assure you, sir, I do assure.

ARMADO: Sir, the King is a noble gentleman, and my familiar, I do assure ye, very good friend. For what is inward between us, let it pass. I do beseech thee, remember thy courtesy. I beseech thee, apparel thy head. And among other importunate and most serious designs, and of great import indeed, too—but let that pass; for I must tell thee it will please his Grace, by the world, sometime to lean upon my poor shoulder, and with his royal finger thus dally with my excrement, with my mustachio; but, sweet heart, let that pass. By the world, I recount no fable: some certain special honours it pleaseth his greatness to impart to Armado, a soldier, a man of travel, that hath seen the world; but let that pass. The very all of all is—but, sweet heart, I do implore secrecy—that the King would have me present the Princess, sweet chuck, with some delightful ostentation, or show, or pageant, or antic, or firework. Now, understanding that the curate and your sweet self are good at such eruptions and sudden breaking-out of mirth, as it were, I have acquainted you withal, to the end to crave your assistance.

HOLOFERNES: Sir, you shall present before her the Nine Worthies. Sir Nathaniel, as concerning some entertainment of time, some show in the posterior of this day, to be rend'red by our assistance, the King's command, and this most gallant, illustrate, and learned gentleman, before the Princess—I say none so fit as to present the Nine Worthies.

NATHANIEL: Where will you find men worthy enough to present them?

HOLOFERNES: Joshua, yourself; myself, Alexander; this gallant gentleman, Judas Maccabaeus; this swain, because of his great limb or joint, shall pass Pompey the Great; the page, Hercules.

ARMADO: Pardon, sir; error: he is not quantity enough for that Worthy's thumb; he is not so big as the end of his club.

HOLOFERNES. Shall I have audience? He shall present Hercules in minority: his enter and exit shall be strangling a snake; and I will have an apology for that purpose.

MOTH: An excellent device! So, if any of the audience hiss, you may cry "Well done, Hercules; now thou crushest the snake!" That is the way to make an offence gracious, though few have the grace to do it.

ARMADO: For the rest of the Worthies?

HOLOFERNES: I will play three myself.

MOTH: Thrice-worthy gentleman!

ARMADO: Shall I tell you a thing?

HOLOFERNES: We attend.

ARMADO: We will have, if this fadge not, an antic. I beseech you, follow.

HOLOFERNES: Via, goodman Dull! Thou has spoken no word all this while.

DULL: Nor understood none neither, sir.

HOLOFERNES: Allons! we will employ thee.

DULL: I'll make one in a dance, or so, or I will play
    On the tabor to the Worthies, and let them dance the hay.

HOLOFERNES: Most dull, honest Dull! To our sport, away.

Exeunt

Scene II

The park

Enter the Princess, Maria, Katharine, *and* Rosaline

Princess of France: Sweet hearts, we shall be rich ere we depart,
    If fairings come thus plentifully in.
    A lady wall'd about with diamonds!
    Look you what I have from the loving King.
Rosaline: Madam, came nothing else along with that?
Princess of France: Nothing but this! Yes, as much love in rhyme
    As would be cramm'd up in a sheet of paper
    Writ o' both sides the leaf, margent and all,
    That he was fain to seal on Cupid's name.
Rosaline: That was the way to make his godhead wax;
    For he hath been five thousand year a boy.
Katharine: Ay, and a shrewd unhappy gallows too.
Rosaline: You'll ne'er be friends with him: 'a kill'd your sister.
Katharine: He made her melancholy, sad, and heavy;
    And so she died. Had she been light, like you,
    Of such a merry, nimble, stirring spirit,
    She might 'a been a grandam ere she died.
    And so may you; for a light heart lives long.
Rosaline: What's your dark meaning, mouse, of this light word?
Katharine: A light condition in a beauty dark.
Rosaline: We need more light to find your meaning out.
Katharine: You'll mar the light by taking it in snuff;
    Therefore I'll darkly end the argument.
Rosaline: Look what you do, you do it still i' th' dark.
Katharine: So do not you; for you are a light wench.
Rosaline: Indeed, I weigh not you; and therefore light.
Katharine: You weigh me not? O, that's you care not for me.
Rosaline: Great reason; for "past cure is still past care."
Princess of France: Well bandied both; a set of wit well play'd.
    But, Rosaline, you have a favour too?
    Who sent it? and what is it?
Rosaline: I would you knew.

An if my face were but as fair as yours,
My favour were as great: be witness this.
Nay, I have verses too, I thank Berowne;
The numbers true, and, were the numb'ring too,
I were the fairest goddess on the ground.
I am compar'd to twenty thousand fairs.
O, he hath drawn my picture in his letter!

PRINCESS OF FRANCE: Anything like?

ROSALINE: Much in the letters; nothing in the praise.

PRINCESS OF FRANCE: Beauteous as ink—a good conclusion.

KATHARINE: Fair as a text B in a copy-book.

ROSALINE: Ware pencils, ho! Let me not die your debtor,
My red dominical, my golden letter:
O that your face were not so full of O's!

KATHARINE: A pox of that jest! and I beshrew all shrows!

PRINCESS OF FRANCE: But, Katharine, what was sent to you from fair
Dumain?

KATHARINE: Madam, this glove.

PRINCESS OF FRANCE: Did he not send you twain?

KATHARINE: Yes, madam; and, moreover,
Some thousand verses of a faithful lover;
A huge translation of hypocrisy,
Vilely compil'd, profound simplicity.

MARIA: This, and these pearl, to me sent Longaville;
The letter is too long by half a mile.

PRINCESS OF FRANCE: I think no less. Dost thou not wish in heart
The chain were longer and the letter short?

MARIA: Ay, or I would these hands might never part.

PRINCESS OF FRANCE: We are wise girls to mock our lovers so.

ROSALINE: They are worse fools to purchase mocking so.
That same Berowne I'll torture ere I go.
O that I knew he were but in by th' week!
How I would make him fawn, and beg, and seek,
And wait the season, and observe the times,
And spend his prodigal wits in bootless rhymes,
And shape his service wholly to my hests,
And make him proud to make me proud that jests!
So pertaunt-like would I o'ersway his state
That he should be my fool, and I his fate.

PRINCESS OF FRANCE: None are so surely caught, when they are
    catch'd,
    As wit turn'd fool; folly, in wisdom hatch'd,
    Hath wisdom's warrant and the help of school,
    And wit's own grace to grace a learned fool.
ROSALINE: The blood of youth burns not with such excess
    As gravity's revolt to wantonness.
MARIA: Folly in fools bears not so strong a note
    As fool'ry in the wise when wit doth dote,
    Since all the power thereof it doth apply
    To prove, by wit, worth in simplicity.
Enter BOYET
PRINCESS OF FRANCE: Here comes Boyet, and mirth is in his face.
BOYET: O, I am stabb'd with laughter! Where's her Grace?
PRINCESS OF FRANCE: Thy news, Boyet?
BOYET: Prepare, madam, prepare!
    Arm, wenches, arm! Encounters mounted are
    Against your peace. Love doth approach disguis'd,
    Armed in arguments; you'll be surpris'd.
    Muster your wits; stand in your own defence;
    Or hide your heads like cowards, and fly hence.
PRINCESS OF FRANCE: Saint Dennis to Saint Cupid! What are they
    That charge their breath against us? Say, scout, say.
BOYET: Under the cool shade of a sycamore
    I thought to close mine eyes some half an hour;
    When, lo, to interrupt my purpos'd rest,
    Toward that shade I might behold addrest
    The King and his companions; warily
    I stole into a neighbour thicket by,
    And overheard what you shall overhear—
    That, by and by, disguis'd they will be here.
    Their herald is a pretty knavish page,
    That well by heart hath conn'd his embassage.
    Action and accent did they teach him there:
    "Thus must thou speak" and "thus thy body bear,"
    And ever and anon they made a doubt
    Presence majestical would put him out;
    "For" quoth the King "an angel shalt thou see;
    Yet fear not thou, but speak audaciously."

The boy replied "An angel is not evil;
I should have fear'd her had she been a devil."
With that all laugh'd, and clapp'd him on the shoulder,
Making the bold wag by their praises bolder.
One rubb'd his elbow, thus, and fleer'd, and swore
A better speech was never spoke before.
Another with his finger and his thumb
Cried "Via! we will do't, come what will come."
The third he caper'd, and cried "All goes well."
The fourth turn'd on the toe, and down he fell.
With that they all did tumble on the ground,
With such a zealous laughter, so profound,
That in this spleen ridiculous appears,
To check their folly, passion's solemn tears.

PRINCESS OF FRANCE: But what, but what, come they to visit us?

BOYET: They do, they do, and are apparell'd thus,
Like Muscovites or Russians, as I guess.
Their purpose is to parley, court, and dance;
And everyone his love-feat will advance
Unto his several mistress; which they'll know
By favours several which they did bestow.

PRINCESS OF FRANCE: And will they so? The gallants shall be task'd,
For, ladies, we will everyone be mask'd;
And not a man of them shall have the grace,
Despite of suit, to see a lady's face.
Hold, Rosaline, this favour thou shalt wear,
And then the King will court thee for his dear;
Hold, take thou this, my sweet, and give me thine,
So shall Berowne take me for Rosaline.
And change you favours too; so shall your loves
Woo contrary, deceiv'd by these removes.

ROSALINE: Come on, then, wear the favours most in sight.

KATHARINE: But, in this changing, what is your intent?

PRINCESS OF FRANCE: The effect of my intent is to cross theirs.
They do it but in mocking merriment,
And mock for mock is only my intent.
Their several counsels they unbosom shall
To loves mistook, and so be mock'd withal
Upon the next occasion that we meet

With visages display'd to talk and greet.

ROSALINE: But shall we dance, if they desire us to't?

PRINCESS OF FRANCE: No, to the death, we will not move a foot,
    Nor to their penn'd speech render we no grace;
    But while 'tis spoke each turn away her face.

BOYET: Why, that contempt will kill the speaker's heart,
    And quite divorce his memory from his part.

PRINCESS OF FRANCE: Therefore I do it; and I make no doubt
    The rest will ne'er come in, if he be out.
    There's no such sport as sport by sport o'erthrown,
    To make theirs ours, and ours none but our own;
    So shall we stay, mocking intended game,
    And they well mock'd depart away with shame.

(Trumpet sounds within)

BOYET: The trumpet sounds; be mask'd; the maskers come.

(The LADIES mask)

Enter BLACKAMOORS *music,* MOTH *as Prologue, the* KING *and his* LORDS
as maskers, in the guise of Russians

MOTH: All hail, the richest beauties on the earth!

BOYET: Beauties no richer than rich taffeta.

MOTH: A holy parcel of the fairest dames

(The LADIES turn their backs to him)

    That ever turn'd their—backs—to mortal views!

BEROWNE: Their eyes, villain, their eyes.

MOTH: That ever turn'd their eyes to mortal views!
    Out—

BOYET: True; out indeed.

MOTH: Out of your favours, heavenly spirits, vouchsafe
    Not to behold—

BEROWNE: Once to behold, rogue.

MOTH: Once to behold with your sun-beamed eyes—with your sun-
    beamed eyes—

BOYET: They will not answer to that epithet;
    You were best call it "daughter-beamed eyes."

MOTH: They do not mark me, and that brings me out.

BEROWNE: Is this your perfectness? Be gone, you rogue.

Exit MOTH

ROSALINE: What would these strangers? Know their minds, Boyet.
    If they do speak our language, 'tis our will

That some plain man recount their purposes.
Know what they would.

BOYET: What would you with the Princess?

BEROWNE: Nothing but peace and gentle visitation.

ROSALINE: What would they, say they?

BOYET: Nothing but peace and gentle visitation.

ROSALINE: Why, that they have; and bid them so be gone.

BOYET: She says you have it, and you may be gone.

KING: Say to her we have measur'd many miles
To tread a measure with her on this grass.

BOYET: They say that they have measur'd many a mile
To tread a measure with you on this grass.

ROSALINE: It is not so. Ask them how many inches
Is in one mile? If they have measured many,
The measure, then, of one is eas'ly told.

BOYET: If to come hither you have measur'd miles,
And many miles, the Princess bids you tell
How many inches doth fill up one mile.

BEROWNE: Tell her we measure them by weary steps.

BOYET: She hears herself.

ROSALINE: How many weary steps
Of many weary miles you have o'ergone
Are numb'red in the travel of one mile?

BEROWNE: We number nothing that we spend for you;
Our duty is so rich, so infinite,
That we may do it still without accompt.
Vouchsafe to show the sunshine of your face,
That we, like savages, may worship it.

ROSALINE: My face is but a moon, and clouded too.

KING: Blessed are clouds, to do as such clouds do.
Vouchsafe, bright moon, and these thy stars, to shine,
Those clouds removed, upon our watery eyne.

ROSALINE: O vain petitioner! beg a greater matter;
Thou now requests but moonshine in the water.

KING: Then in our measure do but vouchsafe one change.
Thou bid'st me beg; this begging is not strange.

ROSALINE: Play, music, then. Nay, you must do it soon.
Not yet? No dance! Thus change I like the moon.

KING: Will you not dance? How come you thus estranged?

ROSALINE: You took the moon at full; but now she's changed.

KING: Yet still she is the Moon, and I the Man.
    The music plays; vouchsafe some motion to it.

ROSALINE: Our ears vouchsafe it.

KING: But your legs should do it.

ROSALINE: Since you are strangers, and come here by chance,
    We'll not be nice; take hands. We will not dance.

KING: Why take we hands then?

ROSALINE: Only to part friends.
    Curtsy, sweet hearts; and so the measure ends.

KING: More measure of this measure; be not nice.

ROSALINE: We can afford no more at such a price.

KING: Price you yourselves. What buys your company?

ROSALINE: Your absence only.

KING: That can never be.

ROSALINE: Then cannot we be bought; and so adieu—
    Twice to your visor and half once to you.

KING: If you deny to dance, let's hold more chat.

ROSALINE: In private then.

KING: I am best pleas'd with that.

(*They converse apart*)

BEROWNE: White-handed mistress, one sweet word with thee.

PRINCESS OF FRANCE: Honey, and milk, and sugar; there is three.

BEROWNE: Nay, then, two treys, an if you grow so nice,
    Metheglin, wort, and malmsey; well run dice!
    There's half a dozen sweets.

PRINCESS OF FRANCE: Seventh sweet, adieu!
    Since you can cog, I'll play no more with you.

BEROWNE: One word in secret.

PRINCESS OF FRANCE: Let it not be sweet.

BEROWNE: Thou grievest my gall.

PRINCESS OF FRANCE: Gall! bitter.

BEROWNE: Therefore meet.

(*They converse apart*)

DUMAIN: Will you vouchsafe with me to change a word?

MARIA: Name it.

DUMAIN: Fair lady—

MARIA: Say you so? Fair lord—
    Take that for your fair lady.

DUMAIN: Please it you,
　　As much in private, and I'll bid adieu.

(They converse apart)

KATHARINE: What, was your vizard made without a tongue?

LONGAVILLE: I know the reason, lady, why you ask.

KATHARINE: O for your reason! Quickly, sir; I long.

LONGAVILLE: You have a double tongue within your mask,
　　And would afford my speechless vizard half.

KATHARINE: "Veal" quoth the Dutchman. Is not "veal" a calf?

LONGAVILLE: A calf, fair lady!

KATHARINE: No, a fair lord calf.

LONGAVILLE: Let's part the word.

KATHARINE: No, I'll not be your half.
　　Take all and wean it; it may prove an ox.

LONGAVILLE: Look how you butt yourself in these sharp mocks!
　　Will you give horns, chaste lady? Do not so.

KATHARINE: Then die a calf, before your horns do grow.

LONGAVILLE: One word in private with you ere I die.

KATHARINE: Bleat softly, then; the butcher hears you cry.

(They converse apart)

BOYET: The tongues of mocking wenches are as keen
　　As is the razor's edge invisible,
　　Cutting a smaller hair than may be seen,
　　Above the sense of sense; so sensible
　　Seemeth their conference; their conceits have wings,
　　Fleeter than arrows, bullets, wind, thought, swifter things.

ROSALINE: Not one word more, my maids; break off, break off.

BEROWNE: By heaven, all dry-beaten with pure scoff!

KING: Farewell, mad wenches; you have simple wits.

Exeunt KING, LORDS, *and* BLACKAMOORS

PRINCESS OF FRANCE: Twenty adieus, my frozen Muscovits.
　　Are these the breed of wits so wondered at?

BOYET: Tapers they are, with your sweet breaths puff'd out.

ROSALINE: Well-liking wits they have; gross, gross; fat, fat.

PRINCESS OF FRANCE: O poverty in wit, kingly-poor flout!
　　Will they not, think you, hang themselves tonight?
　　Or ever but in vizards show their faces?
　　This pert Berowne was out of count'nance quite.

ROSALINE: They were all in lamentable cases!

The King was weeping-ripe for a good word.

PRINCESS OF FRANCE: Berowne did swear himself out of all suit.

MARIA: Dumain was at my service, and his sword.
   "No point" quoth I; my servant straight was mute.

KATHARINE: Lord Longaville said I came o'er his heart;
   And trow you what he call'd me?

PRINCESS OF FRANCE: Qualm, perhaps.

KATHARINE: Yes, in good faith.

PRINCESS OF FRANCE: Go, sickness as thou art!

ROSALINE: Well, better wits have worn plain statute-caps.
   But will you hear? The King is my love sworn.

PRINCESS OF FRANCE: And quick Berowne hath plighted faith to me.

KATHARINE: And Longaville was for my service born.

MARIA: Dumain is mine, as sure as bark on tree.

BOYET: Madam, and pretty mistresses, give ear:
   Immediately they will again be here
   In their own shapes; for it can never be
   They will digest this harsh indignity.

PRINCESS OF FRANCE: Will they return?

BOYET: They will, they will, God knows,
   And leap for joy, though they are lame with blows;
   Therefore, change favours; and, when they repair,
   Blow like sweet roses in this summer air.

PRINCESS OF FRANCE: How blow? how blow? Speak to be understood.

BOYET: Fair ladies mask'd are roses in their bud:
   Dismask'd, their damask sweet commixture shown,
   Are angels vailing clouds, or roses blown.

PRINCESS OF FRANCE: Avaunt, perplexity! What shall we do
   If they return in their own shapes to woo?

ROSALINE: Good madam, if by me you'll be advis'd,
   Let's mock them still, as well known as disguis'd.
   Let us complain to them what fools were here,
   Disguis'd like Muscovites, in shapeless gear;
   And wonder what they were, and to what end
   Their shallow shows and prologue vilely penn'd,
   And their rough carriage so ridiculous,
   Should be presented at our tent to us.

BOYET: Ladies, withdraw; the gallants are at hand.

PRINCESS OF FRANCE: Whip to our tents, as roes run o'er land.

Exeunt PRINCESS, ROSALINE, KATHARINE, *and* MARIA

Re-enter the KING, BEROWNE, LONGAVILLE, *and* DUMAIN, *in their proper habits*

KING: Fair sir, God save you! Where's the Princess?

BOYET: Gone to her tent. Please it your Majesty
    Command me any service to her thither?

KING: That she vouchsafe me audience for one word.

BOYET: I will; and so will she, I know, my lord.

                                                   Exit

BEROWNE: This fellow pecks up wit as pigeons pease,
    And utters it again when God doth please.
    He is wit's pedlar, and retails his wares
    At wakes, and wassails, meetings, markets, fairs;
    And we that sell by gross, the Lord doth know,
    Have not the grace to grace it with such show.
    This gallant pins the wenches on his sleeve;
    Had he been Adam, he had tempted Eve.
    A can carve too, and lisp; why this is he
    That kiss'd his hand away in courtesy;
    This is the ape of form, Monsieur the Nice,
    That, when he plays at tables, chides the dice
    In honourable terms; nay, he can sing
    A mean most meanly; and in ushering,
    Mend him who can. The ladies call him sweet;
    The stairs, as he treads on them, kiss his feet.
    This is the flow'r that smiles on everyone,
    To show his teeth as white as whales-bone;
    And consciences that will not die in debt
    Pay him the due of "honey-tongued Boyet."

KING: A blister on his sweet tongue, with my heart,
    That put Armado's page out of his part!

Re-enter the PRINCESS, *ushered by* BOYET; ROSALINE, MARIA, *and* KATHARINE

BEROWNE: See where it comes! Behaviour, what wert thou
    Till this man show'd thee? And what art thou now?

KING: All hail, sweet madam, and fair time of day!

PRINCESS OF FRANCE: "Fair" in "all hail" is foul, as I conceive.

KING: Construe my speeches better, if you may.

PRINCESS OF FRANCE: Then wish me better; I will give you leave.

KING: We came to visit you, and purpose now
    To lead you to our court; vouchsafe it then.
PRINCESS OF FRANCE: This field shall hold me, and so hold your vow:
    Nor God, nor I, delights in perjur'd men.
KING: Rebuke me not for that which you provoke.
    The virtue of your eye must break my oath.
PRINCESS OF FRANCE: You nickname virtue: vice you should have
    spoke;
    For virtue's office never breaks men's troth.
    Now by my maiden honour, yet as pure
    As the unsullied lily, I protest,
    A world of torments though I should endure,
    I would not yield to be your house's guest;
    So much I hate a breaking cause to be
    Of heavenly oaths, vowed with integrity.
KING: O, you have liv'd in desolation here,
    Unseen, unvisited, much to our shame.
PRINCESS OF FRANCE: Not so, my lord; it is not so, I swear;
    We have had pastimes here, and pleasant game;
    A mess of Russians left us but of late.
KING: How, madam! Russians!
PRINCESS OF FRANCE: Ay, in truth, my lord;
    Trim gallants, full of courtship and of state.
ROSALINE: Madam, speak true. It is not so, my lord.
    My lady, to the manner of the days,
    In courtesy gives undeserving praise.
    We four indeed confronted were with four
    In Russian habit; here they stayed an hour
    And talk'd apace; and in that hour, my lord,
    They did not bless us with one happy word.
    I dare not call them fools; but this I think,
    When they are thirsty, fools would fain have drink.
BEROWNE: This jest is dry to me. Fair gentle sweet,
    Your wit makes wise things foolish; when we greet,
    With eyes best seeing, heaven's fiery eye,
    By light we lose light; your capacity
    Is of that nature that to your huge store
    Wise things seem foolish and rich things but poor.
ROSALINE: This proves you wise and rich, for in my eye—

BEROWNE: I am a fool, and full of poverty.

ROSALINE: But that you take what doth to you belong,
   It were a fault to snatch words from my tongue.

BEROWNE: O, I am yours, and all that I possess.

ROSALINE: All the fool mine?

BEROWNE: I cannot give you less.

ROSALINE: Which of the vizards was it that you wore?

BEROWNE: Where? when? what vizard? Why demand you this?

ROSALINE: There, then, that vizard; that superfluous case
   That hid the worse and show'd the better face.

KING: We were descried; they'll mock us now downright.

DUMAIN: Let us confess, and turn it to a jest.

PRINCESS OF FRANCE: Amaz'd, my lord? Why looks your Highness
   sad?

ROSALINE: Help, hold his brows! he'll swoon! Why look you pale?
   Sea-sick, I think, coming from Muscovy.

BEROWNE: Thus pour the stars down plagues for perjury.
   Can any face of brass hold longer out?
   Here stand I, lady—dart thy skill at me,
   Bruise me with scorn, confound me with a flout,
   Thrust thy sharp wit quite through my ignorance,
   Cut me to pieces with thy keen conceit;
   And I will wish thee never more to dance,
   Nor never more in Russian habit wait.
   O, never will I trust to speeches penn'd,
   Nor to the motion of a school-boy's tongue,
   Nor never come in vizard to my friend,
   Nor woo in rhyme, like a blind harper's song.
   Taffeta phrases, silken terms precise,
   Three-pil'd hyperboles, spruce affectation,
   Figures pedantical—these summer-flies
   Have blown me full of maggot ostentation.
   I do forswear them; and I here protest,
   By this white glove—how white the hand, God knows!—
   Henceforth my wooing mind shall be express'd
   In russet yeas, and honest kersey noes.
   And, to begin, wench—so God help me, law!—
   My love to thee is sound, sans crack or flaw.

ROSALINE: Sans "sans," I pray you.

BEROWNE: Yet I have a trick
    Of the old rage; bear with me, I am sick;
    I'll leave it by degrees. Soft, let us see—
    Write "Lord have mercy on us" on those three;
    They are infected; in their hearts it lies;
    They have the plague, and caught it of your eyes.
    These lords are visited; you are not free,
    For the Lord's tokens on you do I see.
PRINCESS OF FRANCE: No, they are free that gave these tokens to us.
BEROWNE: Our states are forfeit; seek not to undo us.
ROSALINE: It is not so; for how can this be true,
    That you stand forfeit, being those that sue?
BEROWNE: Peace; for I will not have to do with you.
ROSALINE: Nor shall not, if I do as I intend.
BEROWNE: Speak for yourselves; my wit is at an end.
KING: Teach us, sweet madam, for our rude transgression
    Some fair excuse.
PRINCESS OF FRANCE: The fairest is confession.
    Were not you here but even now, disguis'd?
KING: Madam, I was.
PRINCESS OF FRANCE: And were you well advis'd?
KING: I was, fair madam.
PRINCESS OF FRANCE: When you then were here,
    What did you whisper in your lady's ear?
KING: That more than all the world I did respect her.
PRINCESS OF FRANCE: When she shall challenge this, you will reject her.
KING: Upon mine honour, no.
PRINCESS OF FRANCE: Peace, peace, forbear;
    Your oath once broke, you force not to forswear.
KING: Despise me when I break this oath of mine.
PRINCESS OF FRANCE: I will; and therefore keep it. Rosaline,
    What did the Russian whisper in your ear?
ROSALINE: Madam, he swore that he did hold me dear
    As precious eyesight, and did value me
    Above this world; adding thereto, moreover,
    That he would wed me, or else die my lover.
PRINCESS OF FRANCE: God give thee joy of him! The noble lord
    Most honourably doth uphold his word.
KING: What mean you, madam? By my life, my troth,

I never swore this lady such an oath.

ROSALINE: By heaven, you did; and, to confirm it plain,
You gave me this; but take it, sir, again.

KING: My faith and this the Princess I did give;
I knew her by this jewel on her sleeve.

PRINCESS OF FRANCE: Pardon me, sir, this jewel did she wear;
And Lord Berowne, I thank him, is my dear.
What, will you have me, or your pearl again?

BEROWNE: Neither of either; I remit both twain.
I see the trick on't: here was a consent,
Knowing aforehand of our merriment,
To dash it like a Christmas comedy.
Some carry-tale, some please-man, some slight zany,
Some mumble-news, some trencher-knight, some Dick,
That smiles his cheek in years and knows the trick
To make my lady laugh when she's dispos'd,
Told our intents before; which once disclos'd,
The ladies did change favours; and then we,
Following the signs, woo'd but the sign of she.
Now, to our perjury to add more terror,
We are again forsworn in will and error.
Much upon this it is; (*To* BOYET) and might not you
Forestall our sport, to make us thus untrue?
Do not you know my lady's foot by th' squier,
And laugh upon the apple of her eye?
And stand between her back, sir, and the fire,
Holding a trencher, jesting merrily?
You put our page out. Go, you are allow'd;
Die when you will, a smock shall be your shroud.
You leer upon me, do you? There's an eye
Wounds like a leaden sword.

BOYET: Full merrily
Hath this brave manage, this career, been run.

BEROWNE: Lo, he is tilting straight! Peace; I have done.

Enter COSTARD
Welcome, pure wit! Thou part'st a fair fray.

COSTARD: O Lord, sir, they would know
Whether the three Worthies shall come in or no?

BEROWNE: What, are there but three?

COSTARD: No, sir; but it is vara fine,
  For everyone pursents three.
BEROWNE: And three times thrice is nine.
COSTARD: Not so, sir; under correction, sir,
  I hope it is not so.
  You cannot beg us, sir, I can assure you, sir; we know what we
    know;
  I hope, sir, three times thrice, sir—
BEROWNE: Is not nine.
COSTARD: Under correction, sir, we know whereuntil it doth amount.
BEROWNE: By Jove, I always took three threes for nine.
COSTARD: O Lord, sir, it were pity you should get your living by
  reck'ning, sir.
BEROWNE: How much is it?
COSTARD: O Lord, sir, the parties themselves, the actors, sir, will show
  whereuntil it doth amount. For mine own part, I am, as they say,
  but to parfect one man in one poor man, Pompion the Great, sir.
BEROWNE: Art thou one of the Worthies?
COSTARD: It pleased them to think me worthy of Pompey the Great;
  for mine own part, I know not the degree of the Worthy; but I am
  to stand for him.
BEROWNE: Go, bid them prepare.
COSTARD: We will turn it finely off, sir; we will take some care.
Exit COSTARD
KING: Berowne, they will shame us; let them not approach.
BEROWNE: We are shame-proof, my lord, and 'tis some policy
  To have one show worse than the King's and his company.
KING: I say they shall not come.
PRINCESS OF FRANCE: Nay, my good lord, let me o'errule you now.
  That sport best pleases that doth least know how;
  Where zeal strives to content, and the contents
  Dies in the zeal of that which it presents.
  Their form confounded makes most form in mirth,
  When great things labouring perish in their birth.
BEROWNE: A right description of our sport, my lord.
Enter ARMADO
ARMADO: Anointed, I implore so much expense of thy royal sweet
  breath as will utter a brace of words.
                    (*Converses apart with the* KING, *and delivers a paper*)

PRINCESS OF FRANCE: Doth this man serve God?

BEROWNE: Why ask you?

PRINCESS OF FRANCE: A speaks not like a man of God his making.

ARMADO: That is all one, my fair, sweet, honey monarch; for, I protest, the schoolmaster is exceeding fantastical; too too vain, too too vain; but we will put it, as they say, to fortuna de la guerra. I wish you the peace of mind, most royal couplement!

Exit ARMADO

KING: Here is like to be a good presence of Worthies. He presents Hector of Troy; the swain, Pompey the Great; the parish curate, Alexander; Arinado's page, Hercules; the pedant, Judas Maccabaeus.

And if these four Worthies in their first show thrive,

These four will change habits and present the other five.

BEROWNE: There is five in the first show.

KING: You are deceived, 'tis not so.

BEROWNE: The pedant, the braggart, the hedge-priest, the fool, and the boy:

Abate throw at novum, and the whole world again

Cannot pick out five such, take each one in his vein.

KING: The ship is under sail, and here she comes amain.

Enter COSTARD, *armed for* POMPEY

COSTARD: I Pompey am—

BEROWNE: You lie, you are not he.

COSTARD: I Pompey am—

BOYET: With libbard's head on knee.

BEROWNE: Well said, old mocker; I must needs be friends with thee.

COSTARD: I Pompey am, Pompey surnam'd the Big—

DUMAIN: The Great.

COSTARD: It is Great, sir.

Pompey surnam'd the Great,

That oft in field, with targe and shield, did make my foe to sweat;

And travelling along this coast, I here am come by chance,

And lay my arms before the legs of this sweet lass of France.

If your ladyship would say "Thanks, Pompey," I had done.

PRINCESS OF FRANCE: Great thanks, great Pompey.

COSTARD: 'Tis not so much worth; but I hope I was perfect.

I made a little fault in Great.

BEROWNE: My hat to a halfpenny, Pompey proves the best Worthy.

Enter SIR NATHANIEL, *for* ALEXANDER

NATHANIEL: When in the world I liv'd, I was the world's commander;
    By east, west, north, and south, I spread my conquering might.
    My scutcheon plain declares that I am Alisander—

BOYET: Your nose says, no, you are not; for it stands to right.

BEROWNE: Your nose smells "no" in this, most tender-smelling
    knight.

PRINCESS OF FRANCE: The conqueror is dismay'd. Proceed, good
    Alexander.

NATHANIEL: When in the world I liv'd, I was the world's commander—

BOYET: Most true, 'tis right, you were so, Alisander.

BEROWNE: Pompey the Great!

COSTARD: Your servant, and Costard.

BEROWNE: Take away the conqueror, take away Alisander.

COSTARD: (*To Sir Nathaniel*) O, Sir, you have overthrown Alisander
    the conqueror! You will be scrap'd out of the painted cloth for
    this. Your lion, that holds his poleaxe sitting on a close-stool, will
    be given to Ajax. He will be the ninth Worthy. A conqueror and
    afeard to speak! Run away for shame, Alisander.

    (*Sir Nathaniel retires*) There, an't shall please you, a foolish
    mild man; an honest man, look you, and soon dash'd. He is a
    marvellous good neighbour, faith, and a very good bowler; but
    for Alisander—alas! you see how 'tis—a little o'erparted. But
    there are Worthies a-coming will speak their mind in someother
    sort.

PRINCESS OF FRANCE: *Stand aside, good Pompey.*

Enter HOLOFERNES, *for* JUDAS; *and* MOTH, *for* HERCULES

HOLOFERNES: Great Hercules is presented by this imp,
    Whose club kill'd Cerberus, that three-headed canus;
    And when be was a babe, a child, a shrimp,
    Thus did he strangle serpents in his manus.
    Quoniam he seemeth in minority,
    Ergo I come with this apology.
    Keep some state in thy exit, and vanish.

(MOTH *retires*)

    Judas I am—

DUMAIN: A Judas!

HOLOFERNES: Not Iscariot, sir.
    Judas I am, ycliped Maccabaeus.

DUMAIN: Judas Maccabaeus clipt is plain Judas.

BEROWNE: A kissing traitor. How art thou prov'd Judas?

HOLOFERNES: Judas I am—

DUMAIN: The more shame for you, Judas!

HOLOFERNES: What mean you, sir?

BOYET: To make Judas hang himself.

HOLOFERNES: Begin, sir; you are my elder.

BEROWNE: Well followed: Judas was hanged on an elder.

HOLOFERNES: I will not be put out of countenance.

BEROWNE: Because thou hast no face.

HOLOFERNES: What is this?

BOYET: A cittern-head.

DUMAIN: The head of a bodkin.

BEROWNE: A death's face in a ring.

LONGAVILLE: The face of an old Roman coin, scarce seen.

BOYET: The pommel of Caesar's falchion.

DUMAIN: The carv'd-bone face on a flask.

BEROWNE: Saint George's half-cheek in a brooch.

DUMAIN: Ay, and in a brooch of lead.

BEROWNE: Ay, and worn in the cap of a tooth-drawer. And now, forward; for we have put thee in countenance.

HOLOFERNES: You have put me out of countenance.

BEROWNE: False: we have given thee faces.

HOLOFERNES: But you have outfac'd them all.

BEROWNE: An thou wert a lion we would do so.

BOYET: Therefore, as he is an ass, let him go. And so adieu, sweet Jude! Nay, why dost thou stay?

DUMAIN: For the latter end of his name.

BEROWNE: For the ass to the Jude; give it him—Jud-as, away.

HOLOFERNES: This is not generous, not gentle, not humble.

BOYET: A light for Monsieur Judas! It grows dark, he may stumble.

(HOLOFERNES *retires*)

PRINCESS OF FRANCE: Alas, poor Maccabaeus, how hath he been baited!

Enter ARMADO, *for* HECTOR

BEROWNE: Hide thy head, Achilles; here comes Hector in arms.

DUMAIN: Though my mocks come home by me, I will now be merry.

KING: Hector was but a Troyan in respect of this.

BOYET: But is this Hector?

DUMAIN: I think Hector was not so clean-timber'd.

LONGAVILLE: His leg is too big for Hector's.

DUMAIN: More calf, certain.

BOYET: No; he is best indued in the small.

BEROWNE: This cannot be Hector.

DUMAIN: He's a god or a painter, for he makes faces.

ARMADO: The armipotent Mars, of lances the almighty,
    Gave Hector a gift—

DUMAIN: A gilt nutmeg.

BEROWNE: A lemon.

LONGAVILLE: Stuck with cloves.

DUMAIN: No, cloven.

ARMADO: Peace!
    The armipotent Mars, of lances the almighty,
    Gave Hector a gift, the heir of Ilion;
    A man so breathed that certain he would fight ye,
    From morn till night out of his pavilion.
    I am that flower—

DUMAIN: That mint.

LONGAVILLE: That columbine.

ARMADO: Sweet Lord Longaville, rein thy tongue.

LONGAVILLE: I must rather give it the rein, for it runs against Hector.

DUMAIN: Ay, and Hector's a greyhound.

ARMADO: The sweet war-man is dead and rotten; sweet chucks, beat
not the bones of the buried; when he breathed, he was a man. But
I will forward with my device. (*To the* PRINCESS) Sweet royalty,
bestow on me the sense of hearing.

(BEROWNE *steps forth, and speaks to* COSTARD)

PRINCESS OF FRANCE: Speak, brave Hector; we are much delighted.

ARMADO: I do adore thy sweet Grace's slipper.

BOYET: (*Aside to* DUMAIN) Loves her by the foot.

DUMAIN: (*Aside to* BOYET) He may not by the yard.

ARMADO: This Hector far surmounted Hannibal—

COSTARD: The party is gone, fellow Hector, she is gone; she is two
months on her way.

ARMADO: What meanest thou?

COSTARD: Faith, unless you play the honest Troyan, the poor wench is
cast away. She's quick; the child brags in her belly already; 'tis yours.

ARMADO: Dost thou infamonize me among potentates? Thou shalt die.

COSTARD: Then shall Hector be whipt for Jaquenetta that is quick by him, and hang'd for Pompey that is dead by him.

DUMAIN: Most rare Pompey!

BOYET: Renowned Pompey!

BEROWNE: Greater than Great! Great, great, great Pompey! Pompey the Huge!

DUMAIN: Hector trembles.

BEROWNE: Pompey is moved. More Ates, more Ates! Stir them on! stir them on!

DUMAIN: Hector will challenge him.

BEROWNE: Ay, if 'a have no more man's blood in his belly than will sup a flea.

ARMADO: By the North Pole, I do challenge thee.

COSTARD: I will not fight with a pole, like a Northern man; I'll slash; I'll do it by the sword. I bepray you, let me borrow my arms again.

DUMAIN: Room for the incensed Worthies!

COSTARD: I'll do it in my shirt.

DUMAIN: Most resolute Pompey!

MOTH: Master, let me take you a buttonhole lower. Do you not see Pompey is uncasing for the combat? What mean you? You will lose your reputation.

ARMADO: Gentlemen and soldiers, pardon me; I will not combat in my shirt.

DUMAIN: You may not deny it: Pompey hath made the challenge.

ARMADO: Sweet bloods, I both may and will.

BEROWNE: What reason have you for 't?

ARMADO: The naked truth of it is: I have no shirt; I go woolward for penance.

BOYET: True, and it was enjoined him in Rome for want of linen; since when, I'll be sworn, he wore none but a dishclout of Jaquenetta's, and that 'a wears next his heart for a favour.

Enter as messenger, MONSIEUR MARCADE

MARCADE: God save you, madam!

PRINCESS OF FRANCE: Welcome, Marcade;
But that thou interruptest our merriment.

MARCADE: I am sorry, madam; for the news I bring
Is heavy in my tongue. The King your father—

PRINCESS OF FRANCE: Dead, for my life!

MARCADE: Even so; my tale is told.

BEROWNE: Worthies away; the scene begins to cloud.

ARMADO: For mine own part, I breathe free breath. I have seen the
day of wrong through the little hole of discretion, and I will right
myself like a soldier.

Exeunt WORTHIES

KING: How fares your Majesty?

PRINCESS OF FRANCE: Boyet, prepare; I will away tonight.

KING: Madam, not so; I do beseech you stay.

PRINCESS OF FRANCE: Prepare, I say. I thank you, gracious lords,
For all your fair endeavours, and entreat,
Out of a new-sad soul, that you vouchsafe
In your rich wisdom to excuse or hide
The liberal opposition of our spirits,
If over-boldly we have borne ourselves
In the converse of breath—your gentleness
Was guilty of it. Farewell, worthy lord.
A heavy heart bears not a nimble tongue.
Excuse me so, coming too short of thanks
For my great suit so easily obtain'd.

KING: The extreme parts of time extremely forms
All causes to the purpose of his speed;
And often at his very loose decides
That which long process could not arbitrate.
And though the mourning brow of progeny
Forbid the smiling courtesy of love
The holy suit which fain it would convince,
Yet, since love's argument was first on foot,
Let not the cloud of sorrow justle it
From what it purpos'd; since to wail friends lost
Is not by much so wholesome-profitable
As to rejoice at friends but newly found.

PRINCESS OF FRANCE: I understand you not; my griefs are double.

BEROWNE: Honest plain words best pierce the ear of grief;
And by these badges understand the King.
For your fair sakes have we neglected time,
Play'd foul play with our oaths; your beauty, ladies,
Hath much deformed us, fashioning our humours
Even to the opposed end of our intents;

And what in us hath seem'd ridiculous,
As love is full of unbefitting strains,
All wanton as a child, skipping and vain;
Form'd by the eye and therefore, like the eye,
Full of strange shapes, of habits, and of forms,
Varying in subjects as the eye doth roll
To every varied object in his glance;
Which parti-coated presence of loose love
Put on by us, if in your heavenly eyes
Have misbecom'd our oaths and gravities,
Those heavenly eyes that look into these faults
Suggested us to make. Therefore, ladies,
Our love being yours, the error that love makes
Is likewise yours. We to ourselves prove false,
By being once false forever to be true
To those that make us both—fair ladies, you;
And even that falsehood, in itself a sin,
Thus purifies itself and turns to grace.

PRINCESS OF FRANCE: We have receiv'd your letters, full of love;
Your favours, the ambassadors of love;
And, in our maiden council, rated them
At courtship, pleasant jest, and courtesy,
As bombast and as lining to the time;
But more devout than this in our respects
Have we not been; and therefore met your loves
In their own fashion, like a merriment.

DUMAIN: Our letters, madam, show'd much more than jest.

LONGAVILLE: So did our looks.

ROSALINE: We did not quote them so.

KING: Now, at the latest minute of the hour,
Grant us your loves.

PRINCESS OF FRANCE: A time, methinks, too short
To make a world-without-end bargain in.
No, no, my lord, your Grace is perjur'd much,
Full of dear guiltiness; and therefore this,
If for my love, as there is no such cause,
You will do aught—this shall you do for me:
Your oath I will not trust; but go with speed
To some forlorn and naked hermitage,

Remote from all the pleasures of the world;
There stay until the twelve celestial signs
Have brought about the annual reckoning.
If this austere insociable life
Change not your offer made in heat of blood,
If frosts and fasts, hard lodging and thin weeds,
Nip not the gaudy blossoms of your love,
But that it bear this trial, and last love,
Then, at the expiration of the year,
Come, challenge me, challenge me by these deserts;
And, by this virgin palm now kissing thine,
I will be thine; and, till that instant, shut
My woeful self up in a mournful house,
Raining the tears of lamentation
For the remembrance of my father's death.
If this thou do deny, let our hands part,
Neither intitled in the other's heart.

KING: If this, or more than this, I would deny,
To flatter up these powers of mine with rest,
The sudden hand of death close up mine eye!
Hence hermit then, my heart is in thy breast.

BEROWNE: And what to me, my love? and what to me?

ROSALINE: You must he purged too, your sins are rack'd;
You are attaint with faults and perjury;
Therefore, if you my favour mean to get,
A twelvemonth shall you spend, and never rest,
But seek the weary beds of people sick.

DUMAIN: But what to me, my love? but what to me?
A wife?

KATHARINE: A beard, fair health, and honesty;
With threefold love I wish you all these three.

DUMAIN: O, shall I say I thank you, gentle wife?

KATHARINE: No so, my lord; a twelvemonth and a day
I'll mark no words that smooth-fac'd wooers say.
Come when the King doth to my lady come;
Then, if I have much love, I'll give you some.

DUMAIN: I'll serve thee true and faithfully till then.

KATHARINE: Yet swear not, lest ye be forsworn again.

LONGAVILLE: What says Maria?

MARIA: At the twelvemonth's end
　　I'll change my black gown for a faithful friend.
LONGAVILLE: I'll stay with patience; but the time is long.
MARIA: The liker you; few taller are so young.
BEROWNE: Studies my lady? Mistress, look on me;
　　Behold the window of my heart, mine eye,
　　What humble suit attends thy answer there.
　　Impose some service on me for thy love.
ROSALINE: Oft have I heard of you, my Lord Berowne,
　　Before I saw you; and the world's large tongue
　　Proclaims you for a man replete with mocks,
　　Full of comparisons and wounding flouts,
　　Which you on all estates will execute
　　That lie within the mercy of your wit.
　　To weed this wormwood from your fruitful brain,
　　And therewithal to win me, if you please,
　　Without the which I am not to be won,
　　You shall this twelvemonth term from day today
　　Visit the speechless sick, and still converse
　　With groaning wretches; and your task shall be,
　　With all the fierce endeavour of your wit,
　　To enforce the pained impotent to smile.
BEROWNE: To move wild laughter in the throat of death?
　　It cannot be; it is impossible;
　　Mirth cannot move a soul in agony.
ROSALINE: Why, that's the way to choke a gibing spirit,
　　Whose influence is begot of that loose grace
　　Which shallow laughing hearers give to fools.
　　A jest's prosperity lies in the ear
　　Of him that hears it, never in the tongue
　　Of him that makes it; then, if sickly ears,
　　Deaf'd with the clamours of their own dear groans,
　　Will hear your idle scorns, continue then,
　　And I will have you and that fault withal.
　　But if they will not, throw away that spirit,
　　And I shall find you empty of that fault,
　　Right joyful of your reformation.
BEROWNE: A twelvemonth? Well, befall what will befall,
　　I'll jest a twelvemonth in an hospital.

PRINCESS OF FRANCE: (*To the King*) Ay, sweet my lord, and so I take
     my leave.
KING: No, madam; we will bring you on your way.
BEROWNE: Our wooing doth not end like an old play:
     Jack hath not Jill. These ladies' courtesy
     Might well have made our sport a comedy.
KING: Come, sir, it wants a twelvemonth an' a day,
     And then 'twill end.
BEROWNE: That's too long for a play.
Re-enter ARMADO
ARMADO: Sweet Majesty, vouchsafe me—
PRINCESS OF FRANCE: Was not that not Hector?
DUMAIN: The worthy knight of Troy.
ARMADO: I will kiss thy royal finger, and take leave. I am a votary: I
     have vow'd to Jaquenetta to hold the plough for her sweet love
     three year. But, most esteemed greatness, will you hear the dialogue
     that the two learned men have compiled in praise of the Owl and
     the Cuckoo? It should have followed in the end of our show.
KING: Call them forth quickly; we will do so.
ARMADO: Holla! approach.
(*Enter All*)

      This side is Hiems, Winter; this Ver, the Spring—the one
      maintained by the Owl, th' other by the Cuckoo. Ver, begin.

                              Spring

      When daisies pied and violets blue
      And lady-smocks all silver-white
      And cuckoo-buds of yellow hue
      Do paint the meadows with delight,
      The cuckoo then on every tree
      Mocks married men, for thus sings he:
          "Cuckoo;
      Cuckoo, cuckoo"—O word of fear,
      Unpleasing to a married ear!

      When shepherds pipe on oaten straws,
      And merry larks are ploughmen's clocks;

When turtles tread, and rooks and daws,
And maidens bleach their summer smocks;
The cuckoo then on every tree
Mocks married men, for thus sings he:
    "Cuckoo;
Cuckoo, cuckoo"—O word of fear,
Unpleasing to a married ear!

Winter

When icicles hang by the wall,
And Dick the shepherd blows his nail,
And Tom bears logs into the hall,
And milk comes frozen home in pail,
When blood is nipp'd, and ways be foul,
Then nightly sings the staring owl:
    "Tu-who;
Tu-whit, Tu-who"—A merry note,
While greasy Joan doth keel the pot.

When all aloud the wind doth blow,
And coughing drowns the parson's saw,
And birds sit brooding in the snow,
And Marian's nose looks red and raw,
When roasted crabs hiss in the bowl,
Then nightly sings the staring owl:
    "Tu-who;
Tu-whit, To-who"—A merry note,
While greasy Joan doth keel the pot.

ARMADO: The words of Mercury are harsh after the songs of Apollo.
    You that way: we this way.

Exeunt

THE END

A Note About the Author

William Shakespeare (1564–1616) was an English poet, playwright, and actor. Born in Stratford-upon-Avon, he was the son of John Shakespeare, an alderman and glove-maker, and Mary Arden, a woman from a wealthy family. Likely educated at the King's New School, he would have studied Latin in his youth. At eighteen, he married Anne Hathaway, then twenty-six. Together, they raised three children—Susanna and twins Hamnet and Judith. By 1892, several of his early plays had appeared on stage in London. These works, including *Richard III* and *Henry VI*, show the influence of Elizabethan dramatists Thomas Kyd and Christopher Marlowe. He then found success with a series of comedies, such as *A Midsummer Night's Dream*, *The Merchant of Venice*, *As You Like It*, and *Twelfth Night*. By the late 1590s, Shakespeare wrote two of his finest tragedies, *Romeo and Juliet* and *Julius Caesar*, proving his talent and thematic versatility. The beginning of the 17th century marked a turn in his work, ushering in an era often considered his darkest and most productive. Between 1600 and 1606, he produced such masterpieces as *Hamlet*, *Othello*, *Macbeth*, and *King Lear*, all of which are undoubtedly some of the finest works ever written in the English language. In addition to his 39 plays, many of which were performed by his own company at the legendary Globe Theatre, Shakespeare wrote 154 sonnets and three long poems, many of which continue to be read around the world.

A Note from the Publisher

Spanning many genres, from non-fiction essays to literature classics to children's books and lyric poetry, Mint Edition books showcase the master works of our time in a modern new package. The text is freshly typeset, is clean and easy to read, and features a new note about the author in each volume. Many books also include exclusive new introductory material. Every book boasts a striking new cover, which makes it as appropriate for collecting as it is for gift giving. Mint Edition books are only printed when a reader orders them, so natural resources are not wasted. We're proud that our books are never manufactured in excess and exist only in the exact quantity they need to be read and enjoyed.

bookfinity™

Discover more of your favorite classics with Bookfinity™.

- Track your reading with custom book lists.
- Get great book recommendations for your personalized Reader Type.
- Add reviews for your favorite books.
- AND MUCH MORE!

Visit **bookfinity.com** and take the fun Reader Type quiz to get started.

Enjoy our classic and modern companion pairings!